JESUS CAME PREACHING

JESUS CAME PREACHING

CHRISTIAN PREACHING IN THE NEW AGE

GEORGE A. BUTTRICK

Introduction by
Ralph G. Turnbull

BAKER BOOK HOUSE
Grand Rapids, Michigan

Reprinted 1970 by
Baker Book House Company
with permission of
Charles Scribner's Sons

Notable Books on Preaching

Among the helps for the minister and the theological student are the many volumes on preaching and homiletics. On our shelves are the single volumes written by individual men. There are well known series of lectures, such as the Yale or Lyman Beecher given at Yale Divinity School, New Haven, and the Warrack given to the four University Theological colleges in Scotland. Not many today possess full sets of these famous lectures. Earlier works are unobtainable as they are out of print and some cease to appeal. Nevertheless, the preacher who has access to this thesaurus of preaching and homiletics finds much to suggest and stimulate. Because of this, the time is opportune to select and reissue some of the books which have stood the test of time and have proved of abiding value.

It is proposed to issue a selection over the next few years. Not all will be alike. The homiletical techniques will be observed in them, but the emphases will vary. The wisdom and experience of those who have labored in other days may prove of lasting value in many a difficult hour. The particular books have been chosen in the belief that each will minister to the preacher in different moods of the soul. Representative of those which will be selected are:

The Sermon, by R. C. H. Lenski

The Preacher, His Life and Work, by J. H. Jowett

In Christ's Stead, by A. J. Gossip

The Building of the Church, by C. E. Jefferson
The Preacher and his Models, by J. Stalker
Jesus Came Preaching, by George Buttrick
Lectures on Preaching, by Phillips Brooks
The Glory of the Ministry, by A. T. Robertson

"Preaching can never lose its place so long as the mystery and wonder of the human spirit remain" is the judgment of Charles Sylvester Horne, *The Romance of Preaching.* Believing in the supremacy of preaching as God-appointed for the Church, the minister must equip himself for an incredible task of service. One of the causes of failure in the ministry lies in the lack of definite reading and study. These books will serve to spur on the preacher to greater deeds. We need not copy any man, but we can learn from all who have blazed the trail before us. "Who keeps one end in view, Makes all things serve" (R. Browning).

In issuing these volumes it is our hope and prayer that they will help to keep the ideals fresh and the standards from sagging while the vision remains clear. We must "plod on and keep the passion fresh."

RALPH G. TURNBULL

The First Presbyterian Church
of Seattle, Washington

Introduction

George Arthur Buttrick (1892-   )
Jesus Came Preaching

The title of these Yale Lectures is indicative of the kind of speaker who is both author and preacher. Buttrick was nurtured in England within the Congregational Church and later entered the Presbyterian Church in this country. He is best known for his long ministry at the Madison Avenue Church, New York. Since his retirement he has lectured in seminaries and preached to college and university students.

Like others in this series he toiled strenuously with pen and paper. From wide reading in many fields of interest he captured the best from poetry, music, pictures, and theology. These became servants to illumine the eternal truth as he confronted his generation. His craftsmanship in sermon writing and delivery speaks of an intensity of feeling which caught the hearer and worshipper. Buttrick knew how to husband his time in order to produce and maintain the high standard of excellence found in his preaching.

The lectures embody the swift prose of a style akin to his sermonic work. Dullness was not one of his faults and those who heard Buttrick will recall the thrust and stab of burning speech. Here are chapters to quicken the pulse of interest in preaching and stab afresh the lethargic, discouraged heart. And what a title! — at once Biblical and imaginative — from which we learn anew and take courage. From the example of the Master, Buttrick points us to follow his steps as a preacher.

RALPH G. TURNBULL

I AM glad Dr. Buttrick wrote this book—for the world needs these pages. I am glad he chose the subject, "Jesus Came Preaching." What dignity of expression, what floods of thought it suggests. How the very title woos us to the reading as we FEEL the hope that there shall be soul-food in its pages —and that hope is not disappointed.

Pages 84, 85 will be read and reread and pondered thoughtfully by all who desire strengthening of their faith. Who has not experienced the pulling power of "Something wants them"?

Who has not sensed "Beneath the crackling brilliance of American success there lives a pathetic wistfulness," page 137, and

"God pity all the lonely folk with griefs they do not tell, women waking in the night, and men dissembling well," page 119?

"Let the preacher trace that impulse, tendency, desire back to its home in God, who makes men for Himself. Such preaching shall NOT be in vain," page 131.

"The preacher's best offering is the gift of God," page 140.

"Others have dreamed of world dominion; but here was a carpenter dreaming of dominion by His death. If to Jesus the Cross was the winning of the world to God, dare we leave it unproclaimed?" page 202.

"We have no other Gospel but Christ and Him crucified," page 205.

Because of its possibilities of great helpfulness, I am inviting one thousand ministers to a responsive reading and rereading of these pages—and so the book comes to you.

GEO. D. DAYTON.

Minneapolis, Minnesota.

TO

A. G. B.

amoris causa dignissimae datum dedicatum

PREFACE

THE following chapters, carefully revised for publication, were originally given as the Lyman Beecher Lectures on Preaching at the Divinity School of Yale University last April. They are printed with the kind consent and encouragement of the Trustees of the Lectureship. Chapters I, IV, VI and VIII were given, in an early and different form at Gettysburg Seminary also, in the spring of 1930 on the foundation known as "The Doctor and Mrs. Jeremiah Zimmerman Lectures on Effective Preaching."

The reader has full warrant to know by what road and countryside he will travel in these pages, and towards what destination. This is a discussion of Christian preaching. However, let the layman be reassured: primarily it is concerned, not with the preacher's technique, but with his approach to a new age and with the content of his message. In these troublous but quickening times the mood and intention of the Christian pulpit are of greater moment than niceties of manner and method. The first chapter frankly inquires what vantage-place, if any, remains for the preacher in the modern world. The second chapter is determinative— "Is Christ Still the Preacher's Authority?"—for the suc-

ceeding chapters are pendent from it: if that question
has no "yes," they fall. "That speaking one," wrote
Thomas Carlyle of the preacher, "— if only he could
rediscover his word!" This book contends that his
"word" is Christ interpreted as our Eternal Contemporary. Chapters III, IV and V therefore attempt to
sketch the approach and message of the Christian
preacher respectively to the thought-life, the social order, and the new individual of our times. Chapter VI
on "The Craftsmanship of the Preacher" will probably
prove me abysmally ignorant of the craft—since
preaching is in one regard like bringing up children:
we know all about it until we have to do it; then we
know nothing. Chapter VII, on "The Personality of
the Preacher," is in natural sequence to VI, while the
last chapter essays a theme deplorably strange to modern pulpits but never more imperative—"The Preaching of the Cross."

These topics are vital, whatever may be said for their
discussion in this book. They are not merely for the
specialist or technician; and the hope is held that not
preachers only but others who are concerned about the
application of the Christian fact to our day will here
find some light and prompting.

Footnotes are in most instances footpads, so they have
here been placed under duress in the back pages, the innocent with the predatory, that the gentle reader may
travel undismayed. Scripture quotations are from the

American Standard Version except as otherwise specified.

It is a happy burden to acknowledge the help of many friends. The courtesy of authors and publishers has permitted sundry quotations. The annotations will show the wide generosity of this favor; and thanks are hereby proffered. The Reverend Henry Sloane Coffin, D.D., president of Union Theological Seminary, kindly studied the original plan of the lectures and gave valuable counsel. My comrades in daily work, the Reverend Philip Cowell Jones and the Reverend Robert Wyckoff Searle, D.D., have read parts of the manuscript and have willingly borne the extra stint of labor in which the preparation and delivery involved them. The Reverend John Gardner, D.D., of Riverside, California, has carefully revised the "copy" and made helpful suggestions. Mr. William L. Savage, editor of the religious literature department of Charles Scribner's Sons, has been far more than an excellent representative of his craft; he has been almost a collaborator and assuredly a friend. As with an earlier book, my secretary, Miss Elizabeth M. Eliot, has given unsparing labor. Agnes Gardner Buttrick, my wife, has brought gifts of vivifying ideas, sound judgment, and constant encouragement; and has done besides the routine work of preparing the index.

The Faculty of the Yale Divinity School, under whose auspices the Lyman Beecher Lectures are given, and particularly Dean Luther A. Weigle, have shown signal kindness both during the delivery of the lectures and since in urging their publication.

To all these friends gratitude is due and hereby most heartily extended. They are to be acquitted of any folly in this little book and to be largely credited with that advantage which, under the higher Kindness, we trust it may serve.

G. A. B.

The Madison Avenue Presbyterian Church,
New York, N. Y.,
July, 1931.

CONTENTS

CHAPTER ONE

IS THERE ROOM FOR THE PREACHER TO-DAY?

CHAPTER ONE

IS THERE ROOM FOR THE PREACHER TO-DAY?

IN NEW YORK CITY CHURCH buildings are dwarfed by skyscrapers. Here and there a church has been swallowed in an office structure and lives in a commercial stomach, a tenant on sufferance, somewhat as Jonah lived in the whale. That fact may be a portent.

It is a truism that our era is strewn with lay pulpits. In every sober magazine, in many a newspaper and novel, on the lecture-platform and the stage, the preacher (self-installed if not self-ordained) mounts the steps, hurls his anathemas with all the dogmatism alleged to be characteristic of the calling, and brings down his fist with a resounding thump. We could argue thence that there is no danger of the preacher's craft becoming obsolete, but the argument might be a boomerang. With so many lay-pulpits the church may be an expensive luxury. With preachers everywhere why maintain a special order?

Probably the pulpit has never seemed a strong tower; but in our age, with its journals, its "talkies," and its radio all dictating opinion and reporting the gossip of the world, preaching appears to many eyes to have shrunk to a futility. In a daring sweep of prophecy Paul hailed the preacher as God's agent for the saving of mankind: "For seeing that . . . the world through its wisdom knew not God, it was God's good pleasure through the foolishness of the preaching to save them that believe."[1] The prediction was not utterly wild—or you and I would not repeat it nineteen centuries later, nor remind ourselves in a civilization of which Paul could not have dreamed how once he preached to a few slaves in an upper room the strange Gospel of the Cross. But can we to-day share his romantic faith? Does the preacher now impress us as a "legate of the skies"? To many he is a pathetic figure, an anachronism, a stage-joke—an inoffensive little man jostled by the crowd, and wearing the expression of a startled rabbit. With one hand he holds a circular hat on a bewildered head and with the other desperately clutches an umbrella. The crowd pushes him from the sidewalk; the traffic shoots him back into the crowd. Some curse him; a few laugh; most are unaware of his existence.

Preaching has had its heroic ages. In one of the most notable series of Lyman Beecher Lectures, Charles Silvester Horne celebrates the greathearts of the calling.[2] They, and not kings and warriors, have been the real molders of history. The sermons of Isaiah and

Micah outlast the pyramids, outweigh the cargoes of commerce, and cast in shade the acts of parliaments. But time makes ancient good uncouth, dispensing with institutions once deemed indispensable. Ours is a day of fallen kingdoms: the earth is littered with their débris. Is the pulpit also toppling?

I

Let us inquire how preaching arose. Despite the current gibe, preaching is not rooted in the fear that breeds penance—a penance exploited by a clerical cult for its gain—any more than government arose from political graft. Charlatans in the ministry and grafters in politics are barnacles: they did not build the ship. Preaching is rooted in the fact that our race has always been haunted by the sense of Another—Another spelled with a capital "A," from whom primitive tribes fled as from an Arch-Fear; Another to whom Jesus prayed as to the Great Companion:

> That which we dare invoke to bless;
> Our dearest faith; our ghastliest doubt;
> He, They, One, All; within, without;
> The Power in Darkness whom we guess.[3]

Our race has always understood the mood of the African chief who, when asked about his belief in God, replied: "We know that at night-time Somebody goes by among the trees, but we never speak of it." Somebody does go by among the trees. Somebody flames in the dawn and stirs in the tremor of springtime. Somebody lifts a challenge in our conscience, like a banner unfurled. Somebody gleams in our compassion, like a candle lit on a high altar. Somebody goes by in the scientist's quest for truth and in the artist's vision of beauty. Somebody's fingers play harp-music on the composer's silence. Those same fingers close our eyes to pray, and pluck our loved ones away in death. "Somebody"—our dearest faith! Another haunts our human days. We dimly realize that the ground of our life is in Him. In His will is our peace.

Admittedly God is a faith—"our dearest faith." Admittedly God is a doubt—"our ghastliest doubt." Perchance He must be a faith and doubt if life is to keep its courage and knowledge its zest: "Religion," says Donald Hankey, "is betting one's life there is a God."[4] Yet it is a necessary faith, akin to that necessary faith of science that the universe is a universe, that matter and mind swim in a common medium so that matter can be understood of mind. Without that initial assumption science could not live. Without some initial faith in God (some kind of a God, perhaps a God with no better name than "Coherence") we could not live. If we saw the face of an utterly hopeless man it would strike us dead. This "dearest faith" is axiomatic—like human love. Can you prove a patriot's devotion or a saint's compassion? You would not wish to try! Not a million test-tubes in a row with an experiment in each could prove or disprove that you love your children. Love, like this "dearest faith," is its own evidence; its witness is in the very stuff of life. There is a Power, often in darkness, whom we guess. Yet the guess, though only a guess, is stronger to endure than all earth's certainties.

Preaching is grounded in that awareness of Another. Isaiah's impassioned plea for righteousness sprang from his sense of an eternal rectitude: his only hope of success was that his hearers had that same sense, though beclouded while his was bright. Preaching is rooted in the sense of Another. Christian preaching is rooted in the persuasive faith and piercing conviction that in Christ that Other has made known His love and will for mankind. So, since the day of Jesus, our race has said in effect: "There is a mystery encompassing this shadow-show of earth. Ever and again we feel His touch (or think we feel) and hear His footfall. Yet we are busy tilling the reluctant soil, healing bodies, building homes. Man goeth forth to his labor unremittingly until the evening. But we cannot escape the mystery: there is an unseen realm of which this seen world is but the blurred reflection. In Jesus that unseen has come alive. We would see Jesus. We would understand that Book of His people with their strange, redeeming sense of God. Through Him we would have traffic with the eternal. Yet the traffic of earth holds us. But come you," this wistful race says to the preacher, "and we will set you free from other toil. You shall study the Book. You shall listen in the Silence. You shall toil in the fields of the Spirit. Week by week you shall bring us the harvest of the Unseen."

In answer to that need and cry there have always been those who have felt themselves called to that very task . . . "who were born, not of blood, nor of the will of the flesh, nor of the will of man, but of God."[5] The call was not thundered from the sky nor written in letters of fire across the night; it came with a greater compulsion. There have always been those who could not escape the face of Jesus. They found Him in a Book because He was aforetime in their hearts; they knew His Name because they found Him in a Book. For them

> That one Face, far from vanish, rather grows,
> Or decomposes but to recompose,
> Become (their) universe that feels and knows![6]

It was as if a voice said to them (more imperious and far more kind than any audible voice): "You know by every high surmise that the world is Mine. Yet men will not come to Me that they may have life—though their denial is their wilderness. You must bring them to Me. You know that industry is accursed until it makes a Nazareth-shop its shrine. You know that every war is a civil war—a battle between brothers. And you,

you are Mine, shoddy though you know yourself to be. You have seen the light of the knowledge of the glory of God in Me, and you must tell what you have seen."

So preaching arose—by the immemorial if unspoken plea of mankind, and by the response of the few whom, often to their earthly loss, God "whispers in the ear." So preaching will persist: it is rooted in our seeking for God and in His prior seeking of us. The church will change, for the prophet-soul stands above the church to convince it of sin and to summon it to a dangerous mountain-height. The church would change, even if it seemed without blemish; for all things change. But the prophet abides. He is not of man: the sky opens to let him through. He, like the poet,

> . . . in a golden clime was born,
>   With golden stars above;
> Dowered with the hate of hate, the scorn of scorn,
>   The love of love.[7]

2

"But the pulpit is not democratic, and has no place in a democracy"—so the criticism runs. A fatuous charge, sufficiently disproved—since to make the charge is to commit the crime! Is that magazine article democratic? Does any "by your leave" soothe or soften the critic's voice? Is the Chrysler Building democratic— thrusting above our ocean of bricks like a frenzied swordfish? Or, to move into worthier realms, did

Dostoyevsky ask permission to write *The Brothers Karamazov,* or Rudyard Kipling to confess the world's sin and offer the world's prayer in his *Recessional?* Did Beethoven consult mankind about the *Fifth Symphony?* Group discussion has a useful place, but it breaks on history's logic if it tries to silence the prophet's voice or the poet's song. The eternities have always chosen their own man—some Isaiah from his princely home, some Amos from the plough—and his word has not been the group's word. Nor, in this issue, can we ever pool our ignorance to find wisdom.

All life is outgoing—on the level of the iconoclastic magazine as on the level of the Fourth Gospel. Life is like breath: if we hold it we suffocate. Joy cannot be withheld. A telegram announcing the arrival of a first-born son is seldom democratic; it is more than a telegram: it is a rhapsody! Grief cannot be withheld: it rends its garments. The conviction of God cannot be withheld: it bursts any prison. Only a strangely twisted mind can in the same argument justify the world-wide advertising of Ford cars for monetary profit, but condemn the missionary for telling of Christ in terms of healing at risk of his own life. Elemental forces do not smirk and curtsey. The tides do not truckle. The stars do not apologize for invading our sky. There is in the prophet's soul an inevitable swing of the Spirit's tides, an oncoming as of starry hosts—he *must* speak his word. Not that his office can ever be his throne: it is his

altar where life is laid down. Not that it can ever be his
arrogance: it is the conviction of his sin. It is his burden, his doom, and his exceeding joy. "Woe is me . . .
for mine eyes have seen the King."[8] Yet, in great unworthiness, he must tell what he has seen: "for woe is
unto me, if I preach not the gospel."[9]

3

"But the preacher doesn't do anything"—that is the
critic's sharper thrust. Buildings endure, books can be
handled, bread is the staff of life, but words are lost as
soon as spoken. To pour out words—is that a useful
occupation?

Once we were stranded in a Michigan village between trains. The station-master recommended that the
High School Graduation might profitably engage our
time. We went; and, since we have never learned to be
spectator but must always be participant, we suffered
vicarious joys and torments. We were glad in the beam-
ing gladness of the parents. We were distraught and
tongue-tied with the salutatorian, forgot our lines with
the valedictorian, and fell up the steps to receive our
diploma. Soon we were psychologically limp. Then our
eye fell on a banner proclaiming the class motto: that
revived us, as a red flag revives an exhausted bull. We
make it a private hobby to challenge mottoes and
proverbs. Militaristic dogmas, rotarian catchwords, and
advertising slogans are our especial meat; but any prov-

erb will serve. Here was a proverb: "Deeds not words."
We came to embattled life; we moved to the attack.
"Deeds not words"—but words *are* deeds, we said;
as much deeds of the lips as the making of a table is a
deed of the hands. With that initial thrust reinforce-
ments came flocking to the onset. Had not the Greeks
said: "By words alone are lives of mortals swayed"?
Had not Carlyle thundered: "Cast thy word, thy deed,
into the ever-living, ever-working present"? Had not
the apostle James written that the tongue is the bridle
of the horse, the rudder of the ship?—and had he not
given warning: "The tongue is a fire setting aflame the
whole circle of creation with a flame fed by hell,"[10]
a warning so vehement against unbridled words that
his own words slipped the reins? And had not another
voice more quiet and more searching (the *Word* made
flesh) said to us: "By thy words thou shalt be justified,
and by thy words thou shalt be condemned";[11] "Heaven
and earth shall pass away: but my words shall not
pass away"?[12] We could scarcely be restrained from
dashing down the aisle to beseech the graduating class
to reverse the terms of its motto. We returned to the
depot sad that men should let proverbs lead them by
the nose.

Gamaliel Bradford has a book called *Damaged Souls*.
It is a study in certain discredited figures in American
history—John Randolph, Benedict Arnold, Thomas
Paine, Aaron Burr, Benjamin Franklin Butler, and

others. A motley company!—but Mr. Bradford discovers this trait in common: their facility with words. He says the tongue was the most vivid and effective thing about them:

> . . . they used it, one and all, with singular and passionate urgency, to forward their own purposes, to sway men and women, to achieve the conquest of the world.[13]

He points out that their interest in words was not dilettante. They were forthright people intent on compassing the task in hand:

> They were all busy, active, practical men to whom words were tools, no more. But words were ready, handy, terrible tools, and the results these men obtained with them make one more than ever distrustful of the insidious, tremendous, monstrous agency of speech.[13]

Words are "terrible tools." Words are a "tremendous agency." Yet it is said of the preacher's task that it is "just words"! Of course Mr. Bradford's estimate is not strictly true. Words are not "terrible tools"; they are tools, terrible or beneficent. Speech is not "insidious, tremendous, monstrous agency"; it is an agency. It can be made monstrous, or "a winnowing of angel's wings." "Wherefore comfort one another with these words,"[14] says an epistle; for words can be like healing balm. It is sober truth that words born in the soul's silence are among earth's mightiest tools—a brush to paint pictures, a chisel to carve motives, a battering-ram to break down walls of oppression, a compass to guide the traveller, a light to pierce the soul's gloom. For words are personality articulate. They, more than any tool man has made, are freighted with spirit. "Every idle word that men shall speak, they shall give account thereof in the day of judgment."[15] And every noble word that men shall speak shall rise up in that great day to call them blessed.

4

Granted words are a sovereign instrument, it may be argued that the power of the press has made obsolete the pulpit. Printed words can be read, digested, reprinted and bequeathed to posterity. Spoken words are not even arrows shot into the air; for arrows, even if they miss their mark, return to earth and are available for some new endeavor. Newspapers count their congregations in hundreds of thousands. The novelist after the lapse of generations still weaves his spell through the perpetuity of print. Why all this haranguing of sparse congregations? Why this rigmarole of worship, this fever of organization, this maintenance of elaborate buildings? The voice of the preacher is drowned in the roar of the printing press.

This misgiving is not new. Carlyle could say of the church: "Its functions are becoming more and more superseded. The true Church of England, at this moment, lies in the Editors of its Newspapers."[16] Freder-

ick W. Robertson, one of the noblest of preachers, con-
firmed that judgment in a mood of despair. He wrote:
"I wish I did not hate preaching so much, but the
degradation of being a Brighton preacher is almost intolerable . . . all I say and feel is that by the change of
the times the pulpit has lost its place."[16] That jeremiad
is now upwards of a hundred years old; and it was Robertson's photograph that the storekeeper showed to his
customer, confessing that whenever he was tempted by
short-change or short-measure or shoddy goods he went
into the back room to look at the face of a preacher.
Robertson had become his conscience. Yet in a black
moment Robertson deemed his preaching vain!

look !!

Is the average newspaper convincing in the guise of
savior? *The Chicago Tribune,* presumably! Or the
tabloid press; or the white, ennobling publications of
Mr. Bernarr MacFadden! Dispassionate and clear-
visioned observers of the American scene do not find
redemption coming nigh in our newspapers. There are
syndicates which they brand as sinister. At its worst
the newspaper does not purvey news: it peddles a morbid sensationalism and undermines the public good.
At its best the newspaper is still a newspaper: its function is to supply news. Editorials are an appendage:
how many people read them? They are lost in the
shadow of the advertiser. Granted there are fine exceptions to this rule, to which exceptions the nation is in
debt, the preacher may well doubt if even the "sermon

pages" are in the common instance an unmixed blessing. As they appear in the average newspaper, with
their wrenching of words from their context, their dis-
tortion of meanings, their garbling of sentences, their
exploitation of the controversial, the "spicy," and the
cheap, it is more than debatable if they are any proper
medium for the truth of Christ. The church might fare
better without them. However that may be, the daily
press is ungainly in the rôle of prophet. It is "out of
character." Daily happenings are not a gospel. Christ
cannot convincingly be preached except from a whole
heart, and a life unreservedly committed to Him.

As for books, they and preaching are not antithetic.
They are no foe of the pulpit, but a born ally. But, if
choice is to be made, it is a fair presumption that Jesus
could have written books. Instead, "Jesus came preaching."[17] He trusted His most precious sayings to the
blemished reputation and the precarious memory of
His friends. Hosts of scribes had traced on papyri their
interpretations of the Law. Jesus could have followed
their example; thereby He might have saved Himself
much journeying and a violent death. But would we
exchange His cross or our fragmentary record of the
words of the Cross for any treatise He might have
written? Of a truth it is a printed New Testament that
remains, but its vital power is drawn from a word and
a Person. Being spoken, that word was sharp to pierce
where the written word would have made no mark.

The gospel was and is a living impact. "Jesus came preaching"—and wisdom is justified of her children.

5

But what of the radio?—magic word!—and what of the "talkies" and the "movies"? It would pass the wit of man to tell "what of them." There are whim-whams and prodigies with which even the power of words cannot cope. Our day sees the proposal soberly advanced that all preachers except a few may be led into a lethal chamber of desuetude. The few, declaiming at a radio station, can be heard across the land. If public worship is necessary (and why should it be?) the congregation can foregather, look into the sainted eyes of the amplifier, and hear the voice of an oracle. Nay, the "movies" might show his face; and television shall yet make complete our redemption. The radio is the new savior!

In all charity, it must be asked: Who, then, shall save the radio? The virtual monopoly of the air for monetary gain is a startling comment on our American civilization. The very ether, surely part of man's commonwealth, has become commercialized; and Dvořák's *New World Symphony* is given to us by "courtesy" (save the word!) of somebody's washing-machines or somebody else's baked spaghetti. We laugh at the effrontery, but we remind ourselves that "whom the gods destroy they first make mad." Could anything be madder than the middle air populated by jazz, advertising, bedtime-stories, sermons, more advertising, cooking-lessons, symphony concerts, more advertising, and setting-up exercises—with the great god Cash presiding over the bedlam? An instrument potent for our well-being is, in the rampart individualism of our economic chaos (it cannot be called economic *order*), seized by money-shrewdness. The ether becomes private property. Paul declared that the upper air is infested by demons. The idea was not primitive, as we supposed, but only premature.

All caricature aside (and the caricature is not remote from the truth), can the radio be a substitute for the preacher? It may be his ally enabling him to reach the ocean-liner, the hospital-bed, the mountain-camp, the antarctic expedition; and as such it is an opportunity to be improved, and a boon for which to be grateful. But can it ever be the preachers' substitute? Would anyone rather hear Gandhi over the radio than see and hear him in person? It is significant that even the "movies" must stimulate trade through "personal appearances." Imagine some lovelorn swain pledging his heart's devotion by television! Here is the cardinal fact: we are body and spirit. The spirit cannot rightly function in thin air, or through a picture on a screen, or in any other way apart from its body—for soul and flesh have been made "marvellously compact together." We persist in regarding the body as the hindrance or the

foe of the spirit, but the two are correlates and mutuali-
ties. The sword of the spirit is moved only by its hand
of flesh.

> Let us not always say,
> "Spite of this flesh to-day
> I strove, made head, gained ground upon the whole!"
> As the bird wings and sings,
> Let us cry "All good things
> Are ours, nor soul helps flesh more, now, than flesh
>   helps soul."[18]

We are inescapably children of flesh and spirit. The
spirit in the flesh can speak; the spirit without the flesh
is dumb or speaks only in mechanic echo. The direct
impact of life on life, the flash of the eye, the bodily
nearness, the touch of the hand—these are not optional
to full human intercourse. Without these preaching
may be possible—but such preaching will always be
partly deformed: it can never be life. The failure to
realize that body and soul cannot be sundered while we
live, the failure to pay due tribute to "our brother, the
body," is the lurking nonsense in the supposition that
the radio or the "movie" may become our prophet.
"Where two or three are gathered together"—no,
Jesus was not offering a consolation-prize to ministers
confronting empty pews. "Where two or three are
gathered together," or two or three hundred, there is
the spiritual electricity of common worship, there is
the contagion of a good courage, there is the mutual

pleading that flows from presence to presence (spirit in flesh). "For where two or three are gathered together in my name there am I in the midst."[19] We heard a negro preacher pray the other day, and saw him. "Lord," he began, "I'm clumsy-footed in this praying business. But you're to blame, Lord. I've always been clumsy-footed. You took me from behind the plough. . . ." So the prayer went. It was real. It had the accent of Christ. It was not clumsy-footed. It mounted "with wings like eagles." He, presumably, is one of those preachers whom the radio would relegate to the junkheap. But we would rather see and hear him (yea, and any other lowliest brother with a like sincerity, who lived with us and knew our sins and sorrows and hopes) than listen to an anachronous voice—anachronous because it has left its body.

6

But there remains a final and more threatening onset: "The pulpit has lost its authority," the critic says; and his voice is as one pulling the trigger of a death-gun. If, with perverted curiosity, we examine that death-gun we find that it has three barrels. The first says: "The minister is no longer the best-informed man in his community—at least not on more than one or two subjects, and perhaps not on any; and if he presumes to speak as if he were, that pretension will quickly be punctured." The second barrel says: "The appeal to fear has lost all force. A congregation that has passed, if only by proxy, through the poison-gas, slime, and blood of the trenches is not unduly troubled by an imaginary picture of some possible hell; and, in any event, a God who deals main-ly in physical tortures is both lacking in imagination and brutal in nature, and therefore not Godlike." The third barrel says: "The Bible is no longer the final court of appeal. A searchlight has been turned upon its an-thropology, its astronomy, its history and even upon its ethics." Why, with such a three-barrelled blast shot at him, does the minister persist in remaining perpendicu-lar? Common decency requires that he should die! Yet he lives—because every barrel contains a blank car-tridge suitable only for mock manœuvres!

This criticism we may carry back to the fact of Christ. It will be admitted that He "spoke with au-thority." But He did not covet the title of best-informed man in His community. He was not an artist, or sculp-tor, or statesman, or the head of a family. He disowned omniscience: "But of that day and that hour knoweth no one, not even the angels in heaven, neither the Son. . . ."[20] He apparently accepted many current con-cepts. He "was meek and lowly in heart." Yet He spoke with authority.

Again, the primary appeal of Jesus was not to fear. That appeal is valid within limits. Doctors use it, say-ing to the careless or riotous patient: "Flout this law and you will go into damnation, the damnation of a cankered body and a wrath actually arrived." Jesus used the appeal sparingly, within valid limits; but He did not exploit the external threat. He made His plea to a higher kind of fear. Paul urged Timothy to be a "workman that needeth not to be ashamed."[21] Paul might have summoned the celestial police. He might have said: "Act worthily, or the throne of the skies will convict and punish you." Instead he said: "You have your own judgment-court, and it never adjourns." He might have invoked the thunders of Mount Sinai, but instead he warned: "You have your own Mount Sinai. So live that your nature does not rend itself." Paul learned that plea from Christ, whose soul shines behind it like a light. Jesus used love, not fear, as His best weapon. Yet He spake with authority.

Nor did Jesus build on the literal infallibility of a Book. The Sermon on the Mount goes beyond the ethic of the Mosaic Law. Jesus loved the Book. Only a mind saturated in it and reverencing it could have quoted it as He quoted it. But He did not deal in proof texts. He did not use the Old Testament as a thesis in anthropology, or even as an excursion into theology. He found in it the verities of life; yea, He found in it the verities of God. He found, not an impossible certainty of literal fact, but the vital certitude of regnant and compassionate Spirit. He made no false appeal to the Bible. Yet He spake with authority.

What was His authority? The shepherd went back to

his hills and the fisherman to his lake, saying: "Whence hath this Man this wisdom?[22] So gentle He; yet His words are a command." It was the authority of a Life! Truth is not a formula: it is a Life. It is Another spelled with a capital "A." It is the pressure of that "Other" upon the little life of man. If truth were a formula, science might discover it; but because truth is a Life it demands for its discovery our reason at its keenest, our emotion at its purest, our conduct, our will, our all—and then we shall not find truth except as in mercy truth finds us! How can authority be other than a Life? How otherwise can authority command our life? An ethic, a code, a formula, an "ism" cannot sway vital selves. Truth, love, rightness—are they not all the coming of Him with whom we have to do? Jesus was authority because in Him piercingly and persuasively Light broke upon our world. If that authority remains the preacher need not claim omniscience, or falsely use the Bible, or desert the winsomeness of love for the spectre of fear: he is clothed with Light. Light needs no evidence beyond itself. Light is its own credential.

7

Our time on the planet is short. By some mystery, from some eternity, we are thrust on this little swinging ball called "earth" and there bidden to try the adventure called "life." In various tasks men may spell out their little tale of days. They may build ugly and ex-

pensive cities—but cities moulder and become an ant-
heap. They may make themselves a name—but earth's
names are written in sand: the ocean of time rolls up
and washes them away. They may write books—but
books grow yellow with the years, and the last book-
worms are worms in very fact. They may lead armies
—but stern silence falls at length upon the shrieks,
bleeding, and rotten death of war; and to that silence
men of war must give account. They may make comfort and shelter for their fellows—a lamp to light the
home, a table spread, a strong roof-tree overhead, a
smoother pillow in the time of sickness. In sundry
callings men may fill the allotted hand's-breadth of
years; but on all man's work falls the curtain of death
and it is seen no more. The work of man abides and
fructifies only when it is done in love. So history seems
to show; so our faith teaches. So Browning sings in
Love among the Ruins:

> Oh heart! oh blood that freezes, blood that burns!
> Earth's returns
> For whole centuries of folly, noise and sin!
> Shut them in,
> With their triumphs and their glories and the rest!
> Love is best.[23]

In all the tasks of earth, love is best. There was a Man
who forsook the making of tables, doors, and oxen-
yokes that He might tell mankind of God. Tables,
doors, and oxen-yokes—what do they matter now

alongside His telling of God? Now the whole world
says of Him,

> Thou spread'st a *Table* in my sight.

Now the whole world hears Him say, "Take *my yoke*
upon you,"[24] and knows that yoke is life. Now the
whole world listens as He says, "I am the *door*";[25] and
looking through Him, sees—God! Was He useless?
He "came preaching"!

New York's tenements, its multitudinous roar and
rumble, its chasms of bricks, its trains and ships weav-
ing a strange web of earthly days, pall on the spirit;
but Central Park is green with new grass. One glimpse
of green, only one glimpse; then back again to the
bricks and the sadness and the toil. Yet the glimpse is
enough to tell of another world in which the city's life
is set. Encompassing the city is that other world—
deep meadows, the vast wheel of stars, mountain-peaks
white with unmelting snows, rivers singing to the sea,
trees that "lift their leafy arms to pray." One glimpse
only—but in it the assurance of another world. Christian preaching, poor words glimmering with soul, can
give men the glimpse of another world. Men will come
(if the preacher is faithful) from those pleasures without which they might almost be happy, from their business which chokes them with dust, from their gnawing
memory of sin, from the senseless clamor and grasping

of the day; they will come hungering for the glimpse of God. Even one glimpse will save them: they will know there is another Country, with its mountains of rectitude, its rivers of cleansing grace, its deep sky of the ideal life, its little flowers of an agelong mercy. Of all the tasks of earth this Love is best—the Love of God in the face of Christ. Jesus came preaching. Let the preacher count it all joy that he, too, may preach.

CHAPTER TWO

IS CHRIST STILL THE PREACHER'S AUTHORITY?

CHAPTER TWO

IS CHRIST STILL THE PREACHER'S
AUTHORITY?

"IT IS A FAITHFUL SAYING AND
worthy of all acceptation" that apostolic preaching had
but one word—Christ, from whom all other words
derived their life. The night of pagan cults had a thousand stars; the day of the apostles' gospel had but one
Sun. He was Alpha and Omega. There was no other
name in earth or heaven. All their arguments were
clinched, and all their commands were sealed, in Him.
Masters must be liberal—"knowing ye also have a Master."[1] Servants must be faithful—"as unto Christ" . . .
"who emptied Himself taking the form of a servant."[2]
Men must not harshly judge—"for God shall judge . . .
by Jesus Christ."[3] Soldiers of the kingdom must not
falter—"for consider Him that hath endured."[4]

This testing of all worlds by the spectrum-colors of
His soul, who was the one white Light, is a portent
(a miraculous portent if you covet miracles) which later
we shall try to explore. We are just now concerned to
centralize the fact that the first Christian preaching had

for its cloud by day and its fire by night Christ—Him
crucified and Him risen. Paul is made to say in Frederic
W. H. Myers' poem, as all the goodly fellowship of the
apostles might have said:

> Christ! I am Christ's! and let the name suffice you,
>   Aye, for me too He greatly hath sufficed:
> Lo with no winning words I would entice you,
>   Paul has no honor and no friend but Christ.[5]

I

But our age has scant respect for tradition. In music
the masters are ignored, their rhythms beaten into a
tattoo, their haunting sequences abducted and made
drunk. In art likewise a new fashion prevails, whether
good or bad few know, for few can comprehend. In
morals the upheaval is so vast that it seems at times as
if all the roads were gone, all the bridges down, all the
floods let loose. In religion the revolt has swept beyond
the outer earthworks to the very citadel, so that it is
not now a question of dogma (as of some literally infallible scripture) but of the reality of God. Even in
science doubts are raised concerning the validity of
science, and confession now is made that laws and cate-
gories deemed rock-ribbed in objectivity may be in
large measure the impalpable artifices of our mind.

The authority of Jesus has not escaped the onset. He
would not wish to escape. He covets no refuge but the

wide heaven of truth. Some one has called Him "a lonely Figure unassailed." Lonely He is, but no longer unassailed. Nor is His chief battle with the old foes. The new doubt has been raised in the house of His friends. Not the doubt of His existence: that flimsy ghost of scepticism has been laid: a record too resolute and an influence too personal have slain it. This doubt rather: "How can we be sure of anything He said and did?" If this question does not find satisfying answer it will corrode faith like an acid. The Gospel of John, so reverently competent minds agree to tell us, is an "interpretation" of unknown authorship. It is a portrait in oils painted to confront a later age. It may be based on a lost photograph, and it may be painted in the colors of a truth-filled imagination; but it is an "interpretation." It may be a better likeness than the synoptic photographs, but that again is a question. These photographs themselves appear on close scrutiny to have been retouched. It seems, indeed, that they were "taken" through the camera lens of a personal equation. Can we be sure of what He said and did?

A further doubt afflicts us: Supposing we knew incontrovertibly His words and life, are they valid for our day? Primarily He dealt not in philosophical concepts, which, as Plato's concepts have proved, may be above the assaults of time; He dealt rather in concrete instances which are ephemeral. His teaching was not always in the form of ethical principles, which may carry seeds of permanence; it was addressed to specific human need which day by day is of its own kind. He did not peddle universal panaceas: He prescribed for this man or that an individual surgery or balm: the panacea was in Himself. He walked the pathways of a little turbulent land long ago which now we see as in a picture-book. How can parables of tiny fields and far-off battles be authoritative for a machine-age and a new world? Can words addressed to Capernaum in Aramaic sound anything but faint and far when addressed in translation to Los Angeles or New York?

> Comes faint and far Thy voice
> From vales of Galilee;
> The vision fades in ancient shades—
> How can we follow Thee?[6]

Thus we speak, but the facts belie us; as, for instance, this fact: the sharpest criticism of the Church is that its members wear the name of Christ but contradict His life. The world's charge against the Church is not for following Christ but for failing to follow Him. We might have expected the world to say: "Why bestow your liege devotion on so remote and shadowy a Lord?" What the world actually does say is: "You have not been faithful to Him." Is He, then, "remote and shadowy"?—or is He startlingly authoritative? "You are not like Christ," the world complains. But why should any one be like Christ? Why should life be

made conformable to an auto-mechanic in the Cats-
kills? Why, thrice why, should life be made conformable to a Craftsman in the dim-blue hills of ancient Galilee? Yet it must. By the world's tacit admission, it must.
Does He still constrain us? Once men preached with
truth-filled and resistless passion "Christ and Him
crucified." In that zeal Christian preaching arose. It
captured art and empire, philosophy and sacred ritual,
and laid them at His feet as "gold and frankincense
and myrrh." Can we so preach? Must we not so
preach? Is He still our credential and our sovereign
power? It is the pivotal issue.

2

We ask therefore—What is authority? The question
is not moot but vital. To try to answer it is to embark
on a wide sea. In the attempt we might well say with
Breton fishermen: "Our boat is little and the sea is
vast." Yet it should be possible to find, at least in part,
what is authoritative in our experience; and by some
glimmer of words to give hint of that authority to
others.

We set sail with Webster's *Dictionary* as an uncertain
craft: in the course of the voyage we may be rescued by
some worthier vessel—or we may sink. Authority is defined by "old Noah" as, in its primary meaning, "legal
power." But, in the realm of religion, such an authority
—a judgment handed down from a legal throne—is not

an authority: it is a domination that we resent. If authority delivers us to the judge, and the judge to the jailor, and the jailor casts us into prison, then life is a Sing-Sing; and the convicts will rebel so that not even machine-guns can subdue them.

Let us try another definition, and hope that the new start will not be false. "Authority" in its secondary meaning as given by Webster is "government—those exercising power." But in the realm of religion the mere exercise of power is not authoritative: it is tyrannous.

> "O, it is excellent
> To have a giant's strength; but it is tyrannous
> To use it like a giant." [7]

Thomas Carlyle is said to have stood on London Bridge viewing London slums with bitter complaint: "God does nothing." What did Carlyle wish God to do? Sweep away the slums? But slums are in people, and though swept away they would return. Sweep away the people then? God would not appear very Godlike in the act, and, in any event, it would be a drastic remedy. It is doubtful if slaughtering people improves their condition, and Carlyle himself might be caught in the holocaust. What did Carlyle wish God to do? What *could* God do? He could set deep in human clay the dream of a slumless city, pledge men secretly His strength, and call them to a crusade with Him! But *that* kind of authority "old Noah" admits only in tertiary definition: "Power due to esteem; influence of character." *That* kind of authority God had already given to Thomas Carlyle—a dream, a pledge, a spur; but perhaps Carlyle had allowed the dream to sour into bitterness: "God does nothing." If we are to trust to tertiary meanings it might be wise to find a better word than "authority."

We launch our Webster-craft again after two false starts. This time we run up the sail called "certainty." Perchance "certainty" is the word. The definition is: "a fact unquestionably established." But in the realm of religion, as in many other realms, a fact that is unquestionable is a fact uninteresting or coercive. "The angles at the base of an isosceles triangle are equal"— that is a certainty. But, once found, it is not an inspiring certainty. It has elements of life while we are proving it; but, once proven, it becomes dead unless we make it a spring-board for a further leap into the unknown. If we rest content with it, we are under duress; the mind is in a blind alley. "A dead certainty," Doctor J. A. Hutton has written, "is just that—it is 'dead.'" Unquestionable facts, we might add, are hard facts; and if they could be broken they would probably be found to be hollow. The really interesting facts are those not yet discovered. "Our interest's on the dangerous edge of things." Unquestionable facts are stultifying facts unless we use them as a base, a "Little America," for a new expedition into the unexplored. If Mallory had been certain he could climb Mount Everest he probably would not have made the attempt. The quest is as authoritative as the goal—or, rather, *true authority is both quest and goal.* It is not *certainty* we covet so much as *certitude*—certitude adventuring forth to stamp its "invincible surmise" on a recalcitrant earth; inward conviction seeking, yea, and creating, its outward certainties; and finding them only to seek the more! The factor of the unknown gives life its tang. An authority without the factor of the unknown would not be authoritative for us; it would be dead. Our authority must ring

> . . . interminable changes
> On one everlasting Whisper day and night repeated—so:
> "Something hidden. Go and find it. Go and look behind
>   the Ranges—
> Something lost behind the Ranges. Lost and waiting for
>   you. Go!"[8]

3

This dictionary-voyage may have left us stranded, but at least we have garnered some small treasure from the deep. We have learned that a god who thundered his commands and had no other voice would not be godlike, and that we in obeying him would be of servile soul. There is no infallible church: the stern logic of history has a thousand times punctured that absurd pretension; and if there were, such a church, handing down its judgments from a legal throne, would set the teeth on edge. There is no literally infallible book. If there were, it would be very fallible when it had passed through the cloudy medium of our minds; and, in any event, it would "draw a circle premature" round the questing mind and become our prison: it would be a *dead* certainty. Authority (if we must use the word) is itself a paradox. It is compulsion ruling us above the vagaries of our mood and conduct, yet safeguarding our freedom. It is a finality needing no witness beyond itself, yet holding within itself an Unknown by which it provokes our seeking and challenges us to hazardous adventure. *The paradox of authority: a compulsion safeguarding our freedom—a finality challenging us by an unknown.* This view of authority is strikingly in accord with a recent hypothesis of science. We do not depend on science for our evidence—still less on its ever-changing hypotheses. We argue from the self-witness of the spirit under the total impact of life. Nevertheless we are obedient and grateful before all light science can bring or suggest; and it is interesting and perhaps significant to note that Doctor Arthur H. Compton, who has won the Nobel Prize for his work in physics, is reported in *The New York Times* (March 27, 1931) as saying that "the uncertainty principle" is the "cornerstone of modern science." He is quoted as follows:

The new theory takes away the uniformity of the physical world-view as taught by the older science, which is the basis for the so-called mechanistic view of man's consciousness. It leaves room for an effective intelligence behind the phenomena of nature.

At the bottom of physical things there is an element of chance, an essential uncertainty and unpredictability. Man cannot be considered as an automaton in this picture. He must no longer be viewed as blindly obeying fixed, exact laws without any chance to do anything about it. There is some freedom of choice.

The new physics does not regard the universe as atomic chaos, but, on the contrary, has found strong evidence pointing to the existence of "a directive intelligence."

Authority is creative. It is the fecund quickening of life unto the good, the lovely and the true. Authority finds us and says: "I am that I am": then, as it seems to vanish, it says again: "Seek thou me." Authority is at the last known to be—God, the beyond that is within!

> I see the emotion of saints, lovers and poets all
> to be the kindling of some Personality
> by an eternizing passion. . . .[9]

And not of saints, lovers and poets only, but also of scientists and heroes. Lafcadio Hearn has the story of a hero of the Chinese rice-fields during an earthquake. From his hilltop-farm he saw the ocean swiftly withdrawn, like some prodigious animal crouching for the leap, and knew the leap would be the tidal wave. He saw also that his neighbors working in low fields must be gathered to his hill or swept away. Without that second thought so dear to prudence but in a madness

and an exultation he set fire to his rice-ricks and furi-
ously rang the temple bell. His neighbors thought his
farm on fire and rushed to help him. Then, from that
safe hill, they saw the swirl of waters over fields just
forsaken—and knew their salvation and its cost. Such a
deed is its own authority. It is compelling and it is final.
With rare insight Hearn entitles the story, *A Living
God;* and tells us that the people of those rice-fields
used afterward to go to the temple to worship their
neighbor's spirit while he still was with them in the
flesh. Why not? His spirit in that deed was not his
only: it was a bush that "burned with fire and was not
consumed." Yet such a deed, though compelling and
final, is no fetter on the mind's quest and no thwarting
on the soul's adventure. Nay, it provokes to the quest
and sounds a bugle-note of challenge.

Of such fabric is all authority, whether it be that
intangible honor of the mind called by the scientist
"truth" or that rapt vision called by the artist "beauty."
Its warp is an inner compulsion, a needs-must; its weft
is freedom and the hazard of adventure. The fabric is
a cloth of gold, woven by time's flying shuttles, but on
heaven's loom and under the fingers of the Timeless.

4

If authority is a paradox of compulsion and freedom,
we may return to the prior question of the authority of
Jesus. That question can now be made more explicit:

does Jesus meet both terms of the paradox? Is He compulsion and is He quest?

Was Jesus Himself convinced of such compulsion within Himself? We need not enter those lists where scholars tilt to decide if He made specific claim to Messiahship. He redeemed that title as men then used it. If He made no specific claim the reason is clear: men's notions of Messiahship were too earthy, and a spoken claim is of little worth until a tested life has set its seal upon the words. What is clear is that Jesus became conscious of an ultimate purpose in His nature, an axiomatic power, and in that consciousness made assumptions far more convincing than dogmatic claims. "Every one therefore that heareth these words of mine and doeth them"[10]—the assumption being that His sayings are a final decree by which men and nations stand or fall. "Blessed are they that have been persecuted for righteousness' sake." . . . "Blessed are ye when men . . . shall persecute you . . . for my sake"[11] —the assumption being that He and righteousness are of one texture. "Come unto me, all ye that labor and are heavy laden, and I will give you rest"[12]—well might Walter Pater quote that saying to Mrs. Humphry Ward to rebut her denials, and exclaim, "There is a mystery in it." There *is* a mystery in it! How blasphemous or pitiable the saying would sound on any other lips! But on His lips it is music. There is also that startling challenge which He flung at the Sinai-throne of the Mosaic Law: "Ye have heard how it was said of old time . . . but I say unto you . . ."[13]

Mr. John Middleton Murry has recently advanced the notion that Jesus was not sinless. His evidence is that Jesus was baptized of John the Baptist. It is virtually his only evidence, and he begs the question by assuming that baptism was always for "remission of sins." He says:

No man was ever less of a humbug than Jesus. When he went out to be baptized by John, he went out to be baptized for "the remission of his sins." . . . No man despised mere ritual and empty ceremony more profoundly than he. He was baptized for his sins because he had sinned.[14]

A flimsy argument! If Jesus was baptized a sinner because baptism was for remission of sins, then Jesus died a malefactor because the cross was a malefactor's doom. Mr. Murry qualifies his accusation of sin, acknowledging that what Jesus would deem sin another might count almost as holiness. But he persists in the charge:

In his later words, we hear beyond all doubt the voice of one who had known sin.[15]

We forbear the argument. His whiteness of spirit does not need our poor words for defence. Harnack says of Jesus: "He shows no break with His past." There are no spectres of memory darkening His eyes; no pathetic half-confession such as we make when we

say: "I do not claim to be a saint, but—"; no half-confession such as John the Baptist made at that very
baptism when he said: "I have need to be baptized of
thee, and comest thou to me?"[16] The New Testament
hails Him as One "who did no sin, neither was guile
found in his mouth."[17] Christ Himself asked: "Which
of you convicteth me of sin?"[18] It is a most unbridled
writing that declares of Him, "we hear beyond all
doubt the voice of one who had known sin." He con-
sented to the Cross, not because He was a malefactor
but to save malefactors by self-identification with them
—His unshadowed compassion laid alongside their
self-appointed gloom. For that same cause He was
baptized. We can imagine some Father Damien ar-
riving at some modern Molokai and beginning in his
cleanness to rub his limbs with chaulmugra oil. We
can imagine the lepers saying to him: "But we have
need to come to thee, and comest thou to us?" We can
imagine some Mr. Murry standing near and saying:
"He must be leprous, or he would not take the cure."
And we can imagine that new Damien saying: "Suffer
it now. Let me have it so. This is the sign that here and
now in love I make common cause with you. Man's
righteousness is justice. God's righteousness is love. It
becometh us to fulfil *all* righteousness."

Our quarrel with the word "sinlessness" as applied to
Jesus is not that the word is false, but that it is too
small. It does not exceed Him; He far exceeds it. "Sin-

lessness" is a negative term. Jesus was not negative. His virtue was not the absence of transgression. His love burned with so intense a flame that no selfishness could have endured that fire. What we are here intent to urge is that Jesus was conscious of a compulsion and a finality in Himself—a consciousness which, whether or not directly claimed, is revealed by more convincing indirection; and that He held that consciousness radiantly unbroken.

5

And what of those who walked with Him in the flesh? Did they recognize that compulsion in Him? Not explicitly at the first—though from the first His "follow Me" had the ring of glad authority. It would have been counter to His nature (and counter to all true authority) had He made at once imperious claims or ever asked a blind obedience. He chose twelve "that they might be with Him."[19] He was their friend. Perhaps at the first they would have spelled the word thus with a small "f." Yet such a friend! Other men built fences in the wide territory of friendship: they enclosed the Jew but shut out the Gentile, enclosed the righteous but shut out the "lesser breeds without the law." But His circle of friendship was a boundless horizon: it gathered in the Jew and the Greek and the Roman, the apostle and the apostate, Mary of Bethany and that other Mary, John and the man whose devils were legion. Not that any one ever made free with Him. They could not; they said to Him in effect:

> Thou judgest us; Thy purity
> Doth all our lusts condemn,[20]

but they knew that in the act of judgment He would stand with them in their condemnation. Gradually they realized that He was mediating to them a Spirit strong enough to conquer the demons with which they believed the air to be infested; a Spirit strong enough to overcome the threat of death; a Spirit kind enough to absorb their sins into His suffering love. Perhaps at the first they did not call this Spirit, "God." Not at once did Jesus teach them to pray, "Our Father." Very much He never taught them while He walked with them in the flesh: "I have yet many things to say unto you, but ye cannot bear them now."[21] He could have composed vast concertos of the soul, but must content Himself with little roundelays. He could have painted vast canvases of dawn, but, because their eyes were dim, He must draw pictures for children's story-books. Yet they came to know by the impact of His life on theirs a Someone beyond sight and touch: He stood between them and the Eternal as mediator. His death became His revealing: He was with them beyond death. In that darkness His light shone doubly bright; in that silence His voice sounded in accents unmistakable.

Granted that the Fourth Gospel is "interpretation,"

that groping for words in one of its earliest avowals is a true index of the final mood of His disciples: "We beheld His radiance, radiance as of an only begotten from a father, full of grace and truth."[22] "Grace" means the free favor of the Eternal. "Truth" means God, not in shadow or symbol, but in reality. This "grace" and "truth" they found in Him. The words are not theology, save as theology is a profound reflection on a profound experience. Similar reflections were penned before the features of Jesus had chance to dim in fleshly memory. Nor was Paul (some of whose letters were written within twenty or thirty years of the Cross) indulging in the apotheosis characteristic of many lands in that age. Such a deification would have been abhorrent to the Jews whose lips through long centuries had been taught to pray: "The Lord thy God is one God." The Greeks might deify Heracles and the Romans might worship Cæsar—but Heracles and Cæsar were raised by that devotion only to a pantheon which already held many deities, good, bad, and indifferent. To the Jew God was One. To the apostles Jesus, by their experience of Him, was *alone*. Phrase it as we will: for them Jesus had His own relationship with God—and He was as far above a pantheon as the heaven is above the earth. He came to have absolute value for them. The friend (spelled with a small "f") became Friend spelled with a capital "F." They could have said with Eunice Tietjens:

I cannot always feel His greatness,
Sometimes He walks beside me, step by step.
And paces slowly in the ways—
The simple, wingless ways
That my thoughts tread. He gossips with me then,
And finds it good;
Not as an eagle might, His great wings folded, be content,
To walk a little, . . .
But as a simple man,
And I forget.

Then suddenly a call floats down
From the clear airy spaces,
The great, keen, lonely heights of being,
And He who was my comrade hears the call
And rises from my side, and soars,
Deep-chanting to the heights.
Then I remember.
And my upward gaze goes with Him, and I see
Far off against the sky
The glint of golden sunlight in His wings.[23]

Thor among the Norse giants could not drain the
horn that seemed within his compass, for it proved to
be joined to an ocean. Those who walked with Jesus
found they could not plumb the deeps of His nature.
They discovered in His friendship a quality enhanced
by death, and a fathomless ocean of love. One word
is clear in the testimony of those who walked with
Him: "This man speaketh with authority."

6

Thus we come directly to our question: Has Jesus that same compulsion for us—a finality which yet honors our freedom? How strange that we should ask it! There is no picture of Him extant, except the fragmentary record of the gospels. The artists have been haunted by Him and baffled. Their portraits are too effeminate or too uncouth, too indulgent or too stern, too remote or too commonplace. Yet savingly He abides. Those canvases in the gallery of the evangelists fulfil the plot of many an old romance: the One they depict takes life and steps down from the frame to walk and talk with men.

> Shakespeare is dust, and will not come
> To question from his Avon tomb,
> And Socrates and Shelley keep
> An Attic and Italian sleep.
>
> They will not see us, nor again
> Shall indignation light the brain
> Where Lincoln on his woodland height
> Tells out the spring and winter night.
>
> They see not. But, O Christians, who
> Throng Holborn and Fifth Avenue,
> May you not meet, in spite of death,
> A traveller from Nazareth?[24]

His footprints are on every road. Biographies of Him multiply. Kahlil Gibran with his *Jesus*,[25] which reads

at its best almost like a fifth gospel; Bruce Barton with
his Jesus,[26] who was a Man among men, almost a business man among business men; Ellery Leonard rebel-
ling in his fierce poet-soul against Bruce Barton's picture and repainting an early picture of his own: *The
Poet of Galilee;*[27] Upton Sinclair[28] finding in Jesus a
carpenter and a revolutionary ("Comrade Jesus hath
his red card"); Evelyn Underhill[29] writing of the
"flight of the alone to the Alone" and claiming Jesus
for a mystic; J. A. Robertson tracing His psychological
journey;[30] Rittelmeyer writing his *Behold the Man*[31] in
an intensity of worship that now is insight like a sword
and now rapture like a torrent; W. Russell Bowie with
his tribute, lovely, poised, quietly separating the essential from the accidental—*The Master;*[32] and J. Middleton Murry finding in Jesus a "Man of Genius"[14] and
driven despite his scepticism to kneel in homage! What
a various company!—yet all drawn to Him as by some
cosmic magnet. They are but the latest group of His
biographers. There have been others as great or greater
than they—Titian, Tintoretto, and Raphael; Mazzini,
Savonarola, and Ruskin; Dante, Blake, Browning, and
Francis Thompson;—all of them trying vainly yet of
the heart's necessity to trace the features of

That one Face, (which) far from vanish, rather grows,
Or decomposes but to recompose,
Become my universe that feels and knows![33]

We may say that Jesus is only a lay figure on whom creative minds have draped their visions, Himself having lost His distinctive traits in mists of antiquity. We may say it, but the word will not convince. For why should He be inevitably the lay figure? And why should such diverse robes fit Him so well? Moreover, we do not begin with clear ideals and then drape them on a dim and sketchy Christ. That is not the psychological sequence. We begin with nebulous ideals and He endows them with body and breath. Our talk of "principles" is windy talk: principles are hardly recognizable, almost null and void, until they find hands and eyes, lips and heart. Ideals which at first are vague as water finally take form of rock in Him.

Criticisms of Him have passed almost as soon as the breath that made them. "There was none of the artist in Him; He was insensible of beauty" one says—He, who made of all nature a parable, found in sky and lake the sign-language of the Eternal, and traced in the crimson oleanders the pathway of God significantly red! "He made denial of family ties and trampled under His heel the loyalties of birth and country," another hints—He whose stories are tender with love of His cottage-home and His Galilee, and who on the Cross gave His mother to His best-trusted disciple as a last and living legacy! "He taught a slave-morality," it is declared—and so He did and well He did, if by slave-morality is meant the finding of infinitudes in common clay, if by slave-morality is meant the conquest of brute force by a terrible meekness of spirit! "His teaching is negative," another critic urges—His teaching who flung direct challenge at the dark proscriptions of the Mosaic Law, and answered its "Thou shalt not" with His "Blessed are they"! "But it is pitched too high," comes the final complaint—yea, verily, as high as a star which yet shines through every lowly window of earth![34] "But why single Him out from other teachers of religion? Why not leave Him in His niche in history?" some querulous voice persists. We have not singled Him out: He singles Himself out—in love; and no niche in history has ever been able to hold Him.

"But how do we know His faith is final? Buddhism is to the Buddhist what Christianity is to the Christian" —so comes the latest thrust of criticism. How do we know? Perhaps we do not know in "dead certainty," but we do know in invincible surmise. Nor is there need that we should substitute a forum of rival faiths (in strife of tongues multiplying words without wisdom) for our worship in the name of Christ. We need not thus foolishly dispense with the findings of history. The ethnic faiths predated Christ: He was Himself the ultimate flower of Judaism. They have been here longer than He to bid for the suffrages of mankind. That men should have said, "for neither is there any other name,"[35] was not a bigotry or a theology: it was confession that they had tried the clutter of cults with

which their world was filled and found them vain,
and then tried Christ to find Him true.[36] No other
Name has ever won such diverse allegiance—Paul and
Tolstoi, Roosevelt and St. Francis, Grenfell and
Schweitzer. No other face is a "Face like all men's
faces." No other voice speaks to every man "in his own
tongue." If other nations refuse Him at our hands, it is
not because He lacks authority but because our hands
have not been clean. Despite our unclean hands His
purity shines through, and His gospel now is read in
over three hundred different tongues. He has become
mankind's other self. Well might that soldier say: "The
soul stands at salute when He passes by." Well might
that little Chinese girl confess: "I have known Him all
my life, and one day I learned His name."

> This is not He alone
> Whom I have known,
>   This is all Christs since time began
> The blood of all the dead
> His veins have shed,
>   For He is God and Ghost and Everyman.[37]

Thus Mr. Murry makes his confession:

. . . Jesus is more than a teacher of an ultimate wisdom.
. . . Jesus was a teacher who died to save men who would
not listen to his teaching. No other teacher has done that.
And that sets him above and apart from all other teachers.
It does not mean, as some may hold, that he added to the
wisdom of the teacher the blindness of a fanatic. The com-

bination is unthinkable and impossible. It means that to the
wisdom of the perfect teacher in him was added the love
of the perfect brother. There have perhaps been others as
wise as Jesus, but none have had his love. Therefore there
have been none so wise. To be wise and love—this is beyond all wisdom.

. . . The old ways of approach to that life-giving stream
are closed to many modern men. For these I write. We
have to know him after the flesh. There is for us no other
way. But to know him after the flesh is to know him after
the spirit: for we shall find that he was, in very truth, the
ineffable Word made Flesh.[38]

7

Yet He is not merely compulsion or finality: in Him
authority comes clothed in its immemorial paradox.
There is no thwarting of our human freedom. "And
why even of yourselves judge ye not what is right?"[39]
—so He speaks when others offer their careful maxims
or dead rules. His authority is grandly proven in the
fact that He claims no authority except that which we
are freely minded to bestow. We bring our questions to
other teachers and seers, and they answer in dicta il-
luminating and profound. We bring our questions to
Him, and He answers in sharper questions of His own!
Such is His authority: when we bring our little enig-
mas to Him, He makes us forget them in the vaster
challenges which He returns on us. He is willing, yea,
eager to be judged of our poor judgment. "What think
ye? Whom do ye say that I am? Why judge ye not of

yourselves?" He exposes Himself in naked spirit to the light of our dim lamp.

And—at the last—His authority is in His "follow Me!" It is the compulsion of a quest. It is the authority of a venture of faith. It is that touch of madness on the soul which bids us launch out into the deep—into a life of nations such as this blood-bespattered planet has not yet known; into the building of a Church that will put our dingy tabernacles to shame; into a vigil and rigor of prayer before which our perfunctory repetitions will cower in self-loathing. So Mr. Murry again:

The spiritual body of Jesus exists and is immortal. Some make their life-giving contact with it through the Eucharist; for others that contact is impossible. But they, through the effort of making the earthly life of Jesus real to themselves, find their souls possessed by love and veneration for the Prince of men. A fount of living water is unsealed in them.

And it may be that this, and this alone, is the great *Christian* experience, ultimate and eternal, though our ways to it must be our own. Of those ways, we may say this, that if they shall truly bring us to the Jesus who is eternal, they must be ways which do not compel us to make sacrifice of aught we truly believe, and know, and are. . . . He would not have us less than men; and we shall lose nothing by remaining men, of our own century and our own country. At the last we shall greatly gain. We shall look like men, on the man Jesus. He will stand our scrutiny. Keep we our heads as high as we can, they shall be bowed at the last.[40]

The authority of Jesus does not demand of us a blind

obedience. It is its own evidence, yet it invites our scrutiny. He knows nothing of an infallible church with judgments handed down. Nor can the authority of Jesus ever be such as to rob us of adventure: it is not a dead certainty. It says always: "Something hidden: go and find it." It provokes to the hazard. It knows nothing of an infallible Book with inescapably established "facts." We do *not* know exactly what He said and did—and if we knew, that rigid record would become our prison. We do *not* know exactly what He would do and say if He were with us in this generation in the flesh—and if we *did* know, that knowledge might be the death of the mind and the black pit of all our questing. We must find our own answer to the vexed issues of our time. We must find our own proof of God. Yet—not of ourselves. We are not alone. His Spirit persists. We have no thundered command, but we have a "still, small voice." We have no arm of iron to compel, but we have the guidance of His undimmed Eyes. We do not accurately know His words, but we know His abiding Word.

Christian preaching in our day has that one Word from which all other words derive their life. The cults of our day have in their night a thousand stars: our gospel has but one Sun. All *our* arguments are clinched, and all our commands are sealed, in Him. *We* test all worlds by the spectrum-colors of His soul, who is the one white Light:

Yea thro' life, death, thro' sorrow and thro' sinning
  He shall suffice me, for he hath sufficed:
Christ is the end, for Christ was the beginning,
  Christ the beginning, for the end is Christ.[41]

CHAPTER THREE

PREACHING CHRIST TO THE MIND OF TO-DAY

CHAPTER THREE

PREACHING CHRIST TO THE MIND
OF TO-DAY

THE MODERN MIND, IT MIGHT
be said, is not modern; and cannot, in all charity, be
called a mind. Certainly it is not modern in the sense of
being lately informed. Mr. Clarence Darrow in a recent
debate with Mr. Gilbert Chesterton on the subject of
religion accused the church of teaching the literal
word of the Bible. Presumably he believes that a representative church accepts without question the biology
and astronomy of the Book of Genesis. Having erected
that straw figure, he bravely slew it. The mind of the
times is often behind the times; and often it is not a
mind. Its processes of thought are not sternly driven to
logical conclusions. It does not mount daringly into the
measureless sky or try to sound the unfathomed depths.
Some theories advanced in the now sacred name of
psychology are more credulous than the wonderments
of the ages of mythology. In most instances the modern
mind is not an ordered intelligence: it is a prejudice, a

vague desire, a mood, a temper—sometimes a bad temper.

It is ravaged by the disease of immediacy. Adopting the false creed of business, it must "get rich quick." It does not understand that steady burning zeal by which Browning's "Grammarian" pursued knowledge through life, and in death pursued knowledge "like a sinking star" beyond the world's edge:

> Did he not magnify the mind, show clear
> Just what it all meant?
> He would not discount life, as fools do here,
> Paid by instalment.[1]

Our age must have immediate adventure without antecedent toil and hazard, so it gains its adventure by proxy through the "movies." It must have immediate music without the culture of appreciation and without the discipline of training, so it gains its music by proxy through the radio. It must have immediate grace of personality without learning obedience by the things that are suffered, so it attends six lectures in psychology dispensed by some Swazi philosopher. It must have immediate religion. If, therefore, somebody tells us that we may have salvation forthwith if only we will teach our subconscious self to behave by reciting to it a morning and evening formula, that somebody is hailed as a new messiah. And if somebody else solves for us "sudden in a moment" the agelong problem of evil by denying its existence (the agelong travail of mind and heart in respect of evil being but a foolish blunder), that somebody is welcomed as a very prophet. "Things are in the saddle and ride mankind"—more than in Emerson's day. Externalism and immediacy are upon the mind of our age like a plague. The preacher cannot compromise with this mind. But he must meet it; and, if he would illumine it, he must adjust to it. He must, for instance, rigorously clarify his own mind, and learn to speak with pith and pointedness. He must cultivate the visual imagination and make vivid his word.

I

Yet our generation has a worthy mind; and, in more senses than one, it has a mind of its own. Study the photographs of the "gay nineties"—the ladies' hats with feathers nodding romantic challenge to the stars, and the men's Prince Alberts of impregnable respectability. Compare them with the photographs of to-day. Our photographs are soft in contour, their loveliness comes by hint and in a mistiness; but those other photographs are clear beyond cavil, objective, dogmatic. Mental fashions have changed as markedly. Our thinking is in a new climate. It is true that the preacher's message is unchanged and unchangeable; that the gospel is an eternal gospel, from everlasting to everlasting the overture of God to men in Jesus Christ; and, like Him who inscribed it in the ink of His blood, "the same yesterday, to-day and forever." But it is also true that the point of challenge for faith moves as the years move, and that in each generation the immutable Gospel wears some new time-aspect. Isaiah's age needed from him an alternate warning and pleading before its pagan statescraft. Ezekiel was intent on rebuilding a broken altar. Matthew saw the children of a promise blind to the fulfilment of the promise in their midst, and bade them open their eyes. The time of the Fourth Gospelist provoked in him the proclamation of the Logos made flesh. The swiftly passing world discovers in the abiding truth new meanings and undreamed-of treasures. Strange that men who seek the new meaning are suspect to their brethren! They of "the concision" always distrust Paul in his adventuring. By some perversity we insist that the time-aspect of the gospel which our fathers saw is the gospel, that the word of very truth they heard is Truth's whole vocabulary, that the smile or frown which the Eternal Verity wore for them is its only mien. Yet time *does* make "ancient good uncouth." In God "we live and move"—and if we do not move we cannot live.

Therefore our inquiry is this: If the message of the preacher in Luther's day was to assert the right of individual access to God, to declare that the God of the Bible (that is to say, the immemorial God of human insight) is not imprisoned in a hierarchy; and if the duty of the preacher in the nineteenth century was to defend

the soul as it shuddered in the newly found immensi-
ties of time and space—what is *our* message? The war
was a watershed. The weather on this side of it is not
the same as on that other safe and settled side. Moreover, we live in an unprecedented control of natural
forces, on a planet shrunk to the size of a neighborhood, and in an economic upheaval or in that ominous
rumbling that warns of upheaval. We live in the midst
of doubt—doubt that is not miasmic like fog but ag-
gressive like an army with spears. Surely the vast surg-
ings of our day should be for the preacher a summons
to a new urgency. He will still proclaim an eternal
Righteousness—but the proclamation will not be with
power or persuasion unless it is bravely applied to the
case in hand. He will still proclaim an eternal Love—
but the word will be void unless it stoops to carry the
burdens of our day.

We shall try, now, to separate from the complicated
temper of our time certain dominant moods and atti-
tudes. The list will not be exhaustive. Some not here
cited will engage us in later chapters. But here and
now let us single out certain challenges that sound
above the general noise, and ask how the preaching of
Christ can prevail in love against them.

2

The mind of our day is a MIND OF REVOLT. It demands
REALITY, and is resolved on FREEDOM. That statement

needs no marshalling of arguments. Art casts off its
accustomed restraints to become "futurism." Poetry
makes short shift of ancient disciplines and sallies
forth as "free verse." Political theory evolves the
doctrine that laws, government, and police safe-
guards are useless inhibitions on the native splendor
of the human spirit. The rising generation seems to be
out on a mad stampede—the older generation being
plaintively convinced that all in their teens were conceived in disobedience and cradled in rebellion (the
older generation being careful to forget who did the
conceiving and the cradling). On every hand voices are
raised—strident voices, somewhat pathological—bid-
ding us "Be free." The marriage-vow, it is broadly
hinted, is an appendix (often an inflamed appendix)
whose use the social organism has outgrown. "Away
with the trammels of yesterday! Away with stale conventions! Let us live!" Precepts are a prison. Reticence
is as passé as horse-drawn street-cars. What matter the
sanctions and sanctities woven from the pains of a thousand years? What matter the hard-won moral verdicts
of the race? Wisdom has been born overnight in certain novelists and publicists, and the new gospel of
"freedom" is preached with a fervor almost evangel-
istic.

Our question is, how to preach Christ to that mind of
revolt.

Surely He would rejoice in it—at least in many of its

moods. And how quick and generous He would be to honor its worth! He also was in high sense a rebel: "I came not to send peace, but a sword."[2] His battle also was with reaction—with "gray-bearded priests and men who walked decrepitly."[3] His gospel, by His own avowal, was new wine, a heady tumult, which old bottles could not contain. In Him humanity struck tents and marched towards a hazardous unknown. He also was a realist. He was a rationalist in the best meaning of the word; for His life was the most rational fact our befuddled planet has ever known. He was a freethinker —again, in the best interpretation of the title—for His mind was as true and deep as the blue sky, as unfettered as an eagle's flight. He broke with a church that was concerned with ritual but complacent before injustice. He spoke witheringly of the parochial mind. He loved the brittle fact. All this we can say—but have sadly failed to say. Some preachers may be needed to safeguard the bestowals of the past; but others surely are called to venture with the pioneers. Nay, these seemingly opposite tasks, rightly conceived, are but one: the scribe instructed in the kingdom will bring forth from his treasures "things new and old."[4] Is the modern revolt a thing so strange that we should wonder at it? Can we rightly condemn it? As we look out on a planet bitter with grudges and hollow with graves, on an industrialism which sometimes resembles a fratricide, on a church rent in factions yet still professing loyalty to Him who prayed that they might "be one"—can we deny that Victorian rules have been wrong or (if they are right) that we have honored them more in the "breach than in the observance"? The modern mind is generous: it questions, not our loyalty to the rules (though it well might!), but the rules themselves, saying: "If this is the best kind of a world your rules can make, none of your smugly-respectable rules, none of your blood-stained rules for us!" Can we grumble? Ought we to condemn? This may be the new wine—harsh and sour enough now, but perchance rich enough at the last to be poured into the Holy Grail.

But!—there is more to be said. Two kinds of people rebel against man-made rules: some rebel because they are unworthy of the rules, and others because the rules are unworthy of them. And these latter rebel, not because they think the rules unworthy of them, but because they are aware of a law which the man-made rules have betrayed. Antigone, in that drama whose vast light time cannot dim, is shown in rebellion against the rules of the state. Her brother had been traitor to his city and in his treacherous war had lost his life. By order of the city's governor his body was left to rot unburied—as fit indignity for his baseness. But Antigone was resolved to give her brother decent burial. There was a law of love deeper than the shame of treachery and higher than the decree of the state. So she also was condemned to die for disobedience, and to

die by starvation. Seeing her inflexible, the governor
asked:

> And didst thou dare to disobey these laws?

She answered him:

> I did not dream thine edict strong enough
> That thou, a mortal man, should'st overpass
> The unwritten laws of God that know no change.[5]

"The unwritten laws of God that know no change"!
Jesus broke with man-made rules, not that He might
be a roving meteor, but that He might move in the
orbit of a Will. There was a certain Calvinism in Him
and in His teaching. It is our contention in these pages
that anything taught as an "ism" may easily set the
teeth on edge; whereas that same fact upheld as His
life exercises on us a most divine constraint. So with
His Calvinism: "Which of you by being anxious can
add one cubit unto the measure of his life?"[6] Which
of us can turn the moon into green cheese, or change
his parentage at will? There is a law. We are free to
jump from the top of a fifty-story building, but not free
in that jump to cancel gravitation. We are free to close
our eyes and to keep them closed, but not free, if we
keep them closed, to escape the atrophy of the optic
nerve. No man breaks the law; he tries, and the law
breaks him. As with the body, so with the spirit. There
is a law that fleshliness is its own decay; that falsehood

does not issue in joy nor treachery in inward peace. There is a law that "light is sown for the righteous"[7] and that the "meek shall inherit the earth."[8] In these matters also Jesus loved the brittle fact. We stand awestruck as we imagine that Mount Sinai of old, with its thunder-roll and lightning-flash and holy Presence. With better reason might we bow before the Mount Sinai of our own lives. The tablets of flesh are more divine than the tablets of stone. Jesus broke with the shibboleths of His day, not that He might be lawless, but that He might the better obey the law within . . . from which law no man can escape.

We have a small son who, once on a time, was relieved by the doctor of his tonsils. The bribe offered him for taking the anæsthetic bravely was two goldfish swimming in a glass-bowl. The small boy was duly brave, and the goldfish were duly given. "What shall we call them?" we asked. "Tonsils and Adenoids," came the reply. So Tonsils and Adenoids they were baptized, they swimming meanwhile in their waters of baptism. Came a day when Tonsils died (or was it Adenoids?), and we were dispatched forthwith to purchase a successor. The successor was carried home in a tiny carton; and we, ruminating on life in general and on the inhabitant of that carton in particular, spoke to ourself as follows: "This goldfish would be justified in joining the revolt of modern youth. He is not meant to swim in a carton: he is made to swim in a sun-flecked pool. But, supposing he were in such a pool and there rebelled—supposing he said 'This pool has stone-edges and I am against stone-edges'—and supposing he jumped clear of the pool onto the path—and supposing he squirmed on the path and told everybody what a good time he was having now that he was free and in a vaster world . . . would he be free? No, he would be dead." We found therein a parable and resolved that it should be given humble place in this little book. Our jazz-tortured age is wriggling on the path exclaiming that it is having a "perfectly thrilling time"; but it dies when it leaves its God-ordained element . . . and not without that nausea and secret self-loathing which the old theologians called "hell."

Jesus had His own Calvinism—but such Calvinism as our world has not known. He did not call the law a "law." He called the law "God." It *is* living. It is personal enough to constrain our personalities. It is regal; and it is forgiving—for it endures all our failures and returns upon us in red colors when we sin. Jesus could have said with deeper meaning than the Psalmist: "O how love I *Thy* law":[9] it was for Him a Presence and a Friend. And in the law He was free. Only in a law can we be free. Who could be free in a mad and ever-changing topsy-turvydom? Law is life; chaos is death. Kreisler is free in his music. We cannot hear him without seeing a flame burning on a high altar. But he is not free from the law. He must conform with that octave of eight notes which ruled music in Abraham's time. He must, in the discipline of training, "scorn delights and live laborious days." He is not free *from* the law. He is free *in* the law—so gloriously free that he can make wood and glue and silk-strands and cat-gut sing like a choir of angels. Jesus was free—not from the law but in the living orbit of the Eternal—so free that with His own wounded body for violin and a Cross for the bow He made an undying music. This we shall say to the mind of revolt: "If therefore the Son shall make you free, ye shall be free indeed."[10]

3

The mind of to-day is a SCIENTIFIC MIND. Probably we little realize how sharp a line is drawn by the modern mind between science and religion. The scientific side of the line is an honorable realm—the religious side is a jungle of sentiment and superstition. Science is straightforward, unflinchingly real, naked to the eye; religion seems by contrast "such stuff as dreams are made on." Nay, the tangible bestowals of science are more marvellous than the alleged miracles of religion. Religion may say a voice spoke from a cloud; but science has actually made of the whole planet a whispering gallery. Religion may speak of a floating axe-head, but science has built that floating steel-city which we call an ocean liner. Science tells how trailing fire-mist cooled and grew solid, of the lowly origins of life, and the spiral of man's steep ascent; religion speaks of the rib of Adam, the wiles of a serpent, and the plucking of an apple from a tree. Science shows us a universe that in the minutest electron and the mightiest constellation is governed by law; religion speaks of changing the orderly event by prayer. We are aware that the issue thus stated is not fairly stated, but we suspect also that a host of people in our day would accept the statement as just and right. Science to them is critical; religion is gullible. Science is waking life; religion is a dream and sometimes a nightmare. Science is a land of fact and proof; religion is a land where imagination rules and fairy tales satisfy.

Our question again is—how to preach Christ to this scientific mind. We shall not try to show where the realm of science and the realm of religion are contiguous or separated or overlapping (that would be beyond our warrant and far beyond our powers), but rather we shall try to indicate how preaching shall approach a scientific age.

Preaching must be starkly honest. It cannot "beg the question." Sermons have scant place that build on the silent assumption, if not on the spoken assertion, that it "is so" because the Bible "says so." That argument becomes valid only when we show that the Bible reads us even as we read it, that it is a startlingly clear mirror held before the soul of man. There was a day when

Jesus took direct issue with His Bible: "Ye have heard
. . . but I say unto you."[11] He was the scientist of the
soul. He read life with more piercing vision than the
scientist reads the stars. He perceived sequences in life
and in nature, and with a mind like a beam of light He
drew the inference. He made appeal only to the truth;
He did not beg the question. Listen to Him as reverently we may imagine Him to have spoken:

Ye hypocrites, you can discern the face of the sky and of
the earth; but how is it that you do not discern this time?[12]
And why even of yourselves judge you not what is right?
You know what kind of living breeds joy and what kind of
living makes civil war. Judge me by that knowledge! Do
not believe me or disbelieve me because the Church says it,
or because it is written in a Book infallible. Judge me by
the pitiless logic of experience. I say that selfishness shrivels
a man. But do not believe me merely because I say it: look
into the eyes of a miser, look at the lips of a sensualist, look
into your own soul. You can put two and two together in
business. Now put two and two together of a deeper sky
and a deeper earth. Why judge you not of yourselves what
is right?

Preaching to-day must build on that realism of Jesus.

It must build also on His humility. Science has come
to its kingdom by being humble, by sitting down before
the Book of Nature like a little child and spelling out
its message word by word. The preacher must be humble. He may say with conviction as the evangelists have
always said, "I know—I know whom I have believed,"

(for humility is humble just because its truth is great);
but he will the better commend his cause if he frankly
admits the hinterland of mystery which neither he nor
any other man can ever chart or even penetrate on
earth. Many a preacher would win his hearing if, having stated some ultimate question and seeking its answer, he should say frankly, "I don't know."

And is it too much to ask of the preacher that the
faith he teaches shall at least be self-consistent? It may
go beyond reason (the faith of science does that) but
insofar as it lives within reason it need not to be self-
contradictory. A self-contradictory faith is not faith,
but black magic. The Church would never have taught
the dogma of infant damnation if it had honored its
reason (and still less if it had honored its compassions),
for the dogma of infant damnation is inconsistent with
the other dogma of the love of God. The light of our
reason is as God-given as the overflow of our tear-
glands. It is an old command that "thou shalt worship
the Lord thy God with all thy mind." The door of a
church ought to be built high enough so that worship-
pers shall not need to leave their heads outside. Why
should the preacher hesitate to assume the best scientific knowledge of his day? David accepted the astronomy of his time; why should not we accept the best
astronomy and the best anthropology of our time? It
shall still be true for David and for us—whether the
earth is round or flat, made in a week or in unimagined

millennia—that "the Lord is my shepherd." Our plea is this: only a rigorously truth-seeking pulpit can hope to move a scientific age.

But preaching to-day, while it honors the scientific mind, must also challenge it. The pulpit is not a throne: it is an altar—yet its fires are not kindled by any human torch. They flame above all life (above the studio, the factory, the laboratory and the home) to guide men to a sacred place. Preaching must challenge science in the name of that mystery from which science itself derives. Let it be made clear that the ultimate tests of science are not scales or measuring rods or chemical reactions—or even the eyes and ears of the scientist. Two scientists were overheard discussing Einstein's theory of relativity. They admitted that the new theory made obsolete much they had taught as truth. Yet they were not bitter or reluctant, but almost eager, in their welcome to the new teaching (thereby giving theologians a lesson in intellectual etiquette). But why throw out of the window the results of half a lifetime's study? Why not continue to teach what they now suspected might be false? Was it because their eyes would not let them continue, or because a telescope would not let them, or because of some scribbled figures on a page? Nay, it was because they must keep faith with an intangible honor of the mind. That intangible honor, not his laboratory, is the scientist's true home. He also, like the artist, must

. . . contend for the shade of a word and a thing not seen with the eyes.[13]

He also must endure as "seeing Him who is invisible." He also is a celebrant at a high, white altar. For his "shade of a word" yet speaks *in him,* and the "thing not seen with the eyes" looks through his eyes to keep him true.

Preaching must also say without any stammering that the scientific quest is not the only road to truth. It must say, and with no apology for the word, that the eye of reason used apart from its other-eye of emotion, is given over to astigmatism. We do not know a mother's love for us or our own love for our children primarily by means of reason, but by means of emotion. Much of truth we never learn until we translate both our reasoning and our feeling into the deed: "Every one therefore that heareth these words of mine and *doeth* them not" (though He feel them profoundly and reason about them brilliantly) "shall build his house of life upon the sand"![14] The mystic's adoration of Another is not as remote as it may seem from the scientist's quest for Truth—and it may be not less valid. Reason is but one faculty. If reason is abstracted from the personality and made truth's only agent, if the findings of emotion are to be denied, then abstracted reason can deal only in abstractions. Its method must always be fragmentary. Perhaps preaching needs to sound that challenge to an age overwhelmingly dependent on a scientific method. Perhaps preaching needs to say point-blank to science: "After all, you are only playing with abstractions":

> For while the Plough tips round the Pole
> The trained mind outs the upright soul,
> As Jesus said the trained mind might,
> Being wiser than the sons of light,
> But trained men's minds are spread so thin
> They let all sorts of darkness in;
> Whatever light man finds they doubt it.
> They love, not light, but talk about it.[15]

With all insistence on intellectual honesty, let us also be emotionally honest. Scores of young "thinkers" are stifling a fine rapture and a high resolve for the sake of being "scientific"—cutting their wealth of emotion into spaghetti-lengths and arguing about them until they have argued them away! Ether-waves are not the whole truth about a sunset, nor dust about man's life. Perhaps the whole truth about anything is not learned by emotion alone or by reason alone or by the will alone; perhaps the whole truth is learned only by the whole impact of life on the whole spirit of man. Perhaps the method of analysis has led us to a cul-de-sac. Perhaps synthesis—the world's synthesis acting on the spirit's synthesis—is a surer method; and perhaps this total synthesis is best achieved in prayer. Ralph Connor writes of a sky-pilot on a western ranch, and of how a cow-boy in the audience began to quibble with him:

"Of course that's in the Bible, ain't it?" "Yes," said the sky-pilot. "Well, how do you know it's true?" Before he could answer, a ranchman interrupted. "Look here!" he said in tones that would not brook denial. The cowboy looked. "Look here, young feller; how do you know anything's true? How do you know the pilot here's true when he speaks? Can't you tell by the feel? Can't you tell by the sound of his voice?"[16] Truth is not a theory, or philosophy might find it. Nor is it a formula, or science might discover it. Truth is a Life, which only life can know. Truth is a Spirit (Truth, Beauty, Holiness) that is known by the "feel," and evermore beareth witness with our spirits.

There is a further word that preaching to-day must speak to the scientific mind of our age: science itself is dependent for its very life on the good motives of mankind. The germ-theory may be used as an instrument of health or of murder. It has been used for both purposes —for the motives of mankind are variable and mixed. A telescope can be used to reveal the wonders of "the starry deep," or it can be used as Alfred Noyes imagines Italian senators using the telescope of Galileo:

> Many believed
> That all was trickery, but he bade them note
> The colours of the boats, and count their sails.
> Then, in a little while, the naked eye
> Saw on the sky-line certain specks that grew,
> Took form and colour; and, within an hour,
> Their magic fleet came foaming into port.

Whereat old senators, wagging their white beards,
And plucking at golden chains with stiff old claws
Too feeble for the sword-hilt, squeaked at once:
"This glass will give us great advantages
In time of war."

         War, war, O God of love,
Even amidst their wonder at Thy world,
Dazed with new beauty, gifted with new powers,
These old men dreamed of blood.[17]

If the race should fall, like Saul, on a sword which
science has taught us to forge, science itself will perish
in that suicide. Nor will science itself be guiltless, since
no man may wash his hands of responsibility for the
motives that sway mankind. Science alone cannot supply true motives, though in their lack science itself is
under threat of death. Where is the well-spring of high
motive? Where is the answer to those deeper questions
before which the realm of sense-phenomena is but a
moving shadow-show? In a "thing not seen with the
eyes"! In that secret quest called prayer! Science is
noble, but science also derives her strength from hidden
wells whose life-giving stream flows clear in One we
call the Christ.

4

The mind of this age is a SCEPTICAL MIND. In some
ages faith is glorified; in others, doubt. Our age glori-
fies doubt. Scepticism is now an evidence of intel-
lect, while confession of faith betokens a dull wit. We

are sceptical of human nature. We are sceptical of democracy. We are sceptical of great men: therefore we "debunk" every heroic figure and have become masters in the biography of disparagement. We are sceptical even of ourselves (our magazines being gloomy with disillusionment), and we are immensely sceptical of God. Whence came these blank misgivings it will not greatly profit us to ask. They are in part the dark legacy of war. The material wounds of conflict are rather quickly healed: grain-fields whiten and red poppies blow where late there was a shell-pocked wilderness. But spirit-wounds find no swift balm. A grievous blow was dealt our self-respect when we found that civilization, which we had hailed as a foretaste of the millennium, was but a thin veneer to hide our brutishness. Nor do we quickly unlearn the hatred which every warring country teaches. And lies (miscalled propaganda) pumped into the veins of people normally humane remain as a virus in the blood long after peace has been declared. Moreover, externalism dulls the soul to the moving of the Spirit; and sex-obsession is its own curse; and license, miscalled freedom, bequeaths only a self-disgust. But, all these causes aside, doubt is on us— in such darkness as seems the final eclipse of faith.

Now the question, once more, is—how to preach Christ to the sceptical mind. Dogmatism will not serve us, nor any flogging of the mind into an unwilling creed. Well do we recall a Sunday-school teacher of our boyhood who, when confronted with some question of ours which threatened his belief in the Bible, would answer: "Set me down not as a thinker, but as a believer." He got half his wish!—even to boyish minds there was something unseemly in that self-hypnotism. The dogmatic preacher is of poor avail.

Condemnation is a weapon to be sparingly used. It is true that some of our doubt is the scum on the top of unruly conduct—a curdling of the stomach that clouds the mind. Jesus was not slow on occasion to state that fact: "How *can* ye believe, who receive glory one of another?"[18]—their vanity had cankered faith. Nevertheless condemnation was not with Christ a major method.

Sharp rebuttal, the puncturing of doubt's absurd pretensions, is sometimes required of the preacher—and in this also Jesus gives example. There are retorts of His that are like rapier-thrusts. The contention of certain psychologists that religion is only an escape-mechanism merits the reply of ridicule. Man, being homeless and affrighted in a vast universe that is ever blind and deaf to his beseeching, has erected for his comfort the fiction of a King who will honor him and a Father who will shelter him—so we are told. Religion is merely a whistling in the dark to keep up courage, and God is the shadow of an imagining flung across an unfeeling sky. But if man is so hopeless why should he create a decidedly expensive fiction? It would be so much easier to take a painless poison and die! A poor faith may be but a psychological refuge, but all of faith has not been poor. Can a rational mind believe that account does justice to the long record of faith's martyrdoms, from Elijah through John the Baptist to Edith Cavell? Does the Cross impress a rational mind as being an escape from anything—and least of all from fear? Did Jesus die because He wished to cherish an imaginary photograph of a benign old Gentleman (called "God") which He had projected onto the face of the universe? The story that the whale swallowed Jonah, or even that Jonah swallowed the whale, is rigorous science compared with the alleged science of some psychologists. We doubt if Jesus would have answered them. Scorn would have seemed a waste of breath. He would have smiled, we think, and said: "Let them alone. Soon their sleep-walking will end. They will bump into some sharp corner of reality—bruised, but awake. Then they can sleep naturally, and feel better in the morning." Sharp retort has its place, for many of scepticism's most precious theories are tottering walls—one puff of genuine thinking will blow them down. Yet sharp retort is mainly destructive: it can break down tottering walls to clear the ground, but it cannot build a house of radiant faith.

What is the preacher's best message for an age of doubt? If doubt is honest—and much of it *is* honest—the preacher of Christ will greet it in a mood akin to reverence. Many a sceptic to-day honors the old sancti-

ties and is sad to think them dead. He convicts the
new freedom (as it calls itself) of being boring when
it is not nasty, and futile when it is not cheap: he will
have none of it. He walks as a brave stoic through the
half-shadows of a forsaken world, willing to believe yet
unable to believe; and with stark honesty of mind
refusing to believe what he cannot believe. That scepticism by its very honor is its own fine creed:

> There lives more faith in honest doubt,
> Believe me, than in half the creeds.[19]

Nay, the preacher of Christ will not only reverence
such scepticism, but be frank to make it his own confession. Is the preacher immune from sceptic moods?
Why should he pretend that he is? The only way for a
free man to be good is for him to choose goodness in
face of a possible, plausible, and most potent evil. He
must cast the vote of his life for goodness against the
other candidate. Perhaps the only way to hold a faith
is to vote for it against our doubts; perhaps misgivings
are the necessary odds by which belief grows strong
and faith proves its courage. However that may be,
faith is chequered by doubts as forest-ground in sun-
shine is dappled with shadows. Man is born to doubts
as the sparks fly upward:

> With me, faith means perpetual unbelief kept quiet.[20]

Was Jesus free from the inrush of doubt threatening
to overwhelm faith? Not if He genuinely shared our

nature! Did He never fear that God might prove at the last an immense nothing dwelling in nowhere? Was not that paralyzing fear a dread ingredient of the "cup" which He prayed might "pass"? Surely He hath borne our doubts and carried our misgivings! Preaching will win the heart of the doubter (though it may not at once clarify his mind) if it shall say: "I know the force of that onset. I also have prayed: 'Lord, I believe; help Thou mine unbelief.'[21] Jesus knows it, too. Look at Him, and you will see."

Then preaching may affirm in glad conviction that if faith is chequered by doubt, doubt also is chequered by faith. Just when we have resolved to believe nothing, since there is nothing to believe,

> Just when we're safest, there's a sunset touch,[20]

and faith comes back to worship at an ancient altar. Not for long can any man escape God! The questionnaire circulated among English-speaking armies during the war showed that "not five men in a thousand have any real doubt of God's existence." It defined the inchoate faith of that cross-section of humanity as follows:

There is something going on in the world which demands primarily allegiance. At the Front men hardly know what it is. . . . They only know—a wonderful majority of them—that something great and righteous wants them and requires of them their help.[22]

Mark you, "something wants them." A fiction of their own creation could not want them. The instigation of the experience was *there* rather than *here;* it was in some unknown, in some eternity. Beauty wants the artist and requires of him his help. He does not concoct beauty in some little studio behind his eyes: that notion would be blasphemy. Beauty pursues him more urgently than he ever can seek Beauty. The social ideal beckons imperiously to men like Mazzini or Rauschenbusch or Grenfell. It is not their invention. It wears that dual aspect that all great experience wears—it is theirs, yet not theirs. It beckons them despite their protest and at cost of their pain. So the scientist pursues Truth. But Truth is not his petty devising: Truth pursues him, compelling him to renounce theories that do not square with facts! There *is* something great and righteous that "wants us." There *is* something "going on in the world which demands primary allegiance." Yet—why call it "something"? It is assuredly and most compellingly alive. It is personal enough to plead with our personal mind and will. It is Beauty for the poet; Truth for the scientist; Righteousness for the moralist; Commonwealth of Man for the social idealist; yea, it is Honesty of Mind for the sceptic; and it is God for all of us. The sceptic also shall say:

> I fled Him, down the nights and down the days;
> I fled Him, down the arches of the years;
> I fled Him, down the labyrinthine ways

Of my own mind; and in the midst of tears
I hid from Him, and under running laughter . . .
From those strong Feet that followed, followed after.

But with unhurrying chase
And unperturbèd pace
Deliberate speed, majestic instancy
They beat—and a Voice beat
More instant than the Feet—
'All things betray thee, who betrayest Me!'[23]

Great preaching does not tell men what to believe.
It shows them, by a gracious sifting of the heart, what
they already believe. It sets the innate faith against the
tortured doubt—and sounds the challenge:

Like you this Christianity or not?
It may be false, but will you wish it true?
Has it your vote to be so if it can?[20]

It declares that the real issue in life is not an issue for
the mind as between faith and doubt (for we all have
doubt and we all have faith, and faith can be shown to
be at least as reasonable as doubt); it is an issue for the
will—an issue as between courage and cowardice. Faith
is at last a venture. No man can find faith by waiting
for certainty. He *has* faith in the midst of his doubts.
Now he must vote for his faith (and why should he
not?—for it is at least the positive thing in him, the
radiant thing, the dangerous thing!); now he must
venture on his faith, burning all his boats and bridges
behind him. Only so can he prove his faith.

Meanwhile there is Jesus in whom that "something great and righteous which demands primary allegiance" seems to have taken flesh, in whom that "Something" seems to abide as an inescapable Presence. There is Jesus who Himself "fought the spectres of the mind, and slew them," who cast His vote for God even against the hazard of the Cross, and who said: "Be of good cheer; I have overcome the world."[24] He is Lord also of the mind, and for an age of doubt He abides the One Gospel.

CHAPTER FOUR

PREACHING CHRIST TO THE SOCIAL ORDER

CHAPTER FOUR

PREACHING CHRIST TO THE SOCIAL ORDER

THE QUESTION FOR THIS
chapter is—ought we to preach to the social need?—
and, if there *is* distinctively a social gospel, *how* shall
it be proclaimed? The question maroons us in No
Man's Land. On one side are the trenches of those who
bid us "stick to the gospel." It is reported of Lord Mel-
bourne, the British Prime Minister, that he stamped
angrily from his church during an evangelical revival,
shouting: "This has come to a pretty pass when religion
is made to invade the sphere of private life." His gospel
must not be caught trespassing in the walled garden of
daily conduct, let alone on that still more private territory of trade and politics; it must be preached *in vacuo*.
Thus the extremists of one party. On the other side are
the trenches of those who avow that the very essence of
the gospel is an ethical demand and a social crusade.
Consider this extract from a letter which reached us just
before Easter Sunday. It came from a progressive labor
group, requesting that we read a message from them to
the Easter congregation concerning the crimes of capi-

tal in the West Virginia coal-mines. Two paragraphs from the letter run as follows:

If there be anything more important for those who claim to reverence the Carpenter of Nazareth to consider on a great festival day than the issues raised in the accompanying address, we cannot imagine what it is. Was it not during a similar festival season that he challenged the privileged and the powerful of his own day, overthrew the tables of the money changers, and pronounced woe upon those "who offend one of these little ones"?

We have no desire to create any unseemly disturbance. If bringing issues such as this forward for consideration by supposedly Christian, civilized American citizens in the midst of religious exercises be in itself disturbing, then we should deem that a reflection on what passes for religion in our day rather than upon us or upon the workers whom we represent.

Truly this topic is a No Man's Land with no hiding place save the shell-holes made by missiles aimed at those who have been earlier victims. The cross-fire is withering; but, if one can survive it, No Man's Land is a strategic place from which to view the opposing trenches.

For ourself, we have never been able to regard the gospel as concerned with a vague entity called "the soul" and with nothing else. We do not expect to meet (at least in this life) a soul except as the invisible tenant of a body. Nor have we been able to regard the gospel as merely "individualistic": We do not expect to see an individual who is not inevitably shaping other individuals and being shaped by them. The gospel is not a squirrel-cage of pious platitudes. It is not some abstract principle which at the hands of the preacher must move at stellar distance from present and practical application. It is not an innocuous orthodoxy to be taken for a Sabbath airing in the ecclesiastical baby-buggy. It is for all of life. If it is for only part of life (for the "hereafter" but not for the "here," for the man but not for his world) the gospel itself is doomed: a better gospel will supersede it. Doctor A. B. Belden has written: "If religion ends with the individual, it ends."[1] Is Jesus Himself our gospel? But He came with such sharp challenge to His age that they hung Him by the hands and feet until He died.

I

We need not overstate this aspect of the case, but we must state it. The social teachings of Jesus can so be stressed as to make Him no more than a social reformer, rather than One whose words are eternal verities, and whose life and death have a cosmic sway. It might be argued, and with real evidence for support, that Jesus in the days of His flesh was hampered by the social gospel. There were people who tried to make Him a crusader against the iniquitous domination of Rome, to use Him as a red flag or a party cry. He refused the attempt, but it remained as a fetter on His rightful mission. There are sociologists in the church who leave the impression that they are sociologists before they are Christian. Their loyalty is to a movement or an "ism" rather than to a Person. They treat the gospel as though it were a somewhat desirable ally of an economic theory. It is reported of the King of England that, when it was suggested that he, presumably a conservative, would not welcome nor co-operate with the Labor Government chosen by his subjects, he replied grandly: "I would have you understand that no political party has me in its pocket." No political party, socialistic or otherwise, can ever have Jesus in its pocket. He is no mere partisan or reformer. But, on the other hand, the social teachings of Jesus can be so ignored as to leave His message in a vacuum, shorn of its revolutionary meanings. Mortal life is a duality in two regards. It is a duality in that spirit is linked with matter or body, matter being at once the limitation and the agency of spirit. (Science and philosophy may sometime resolve that duality, but the day is not yet.) It is a duality also in that the individual is fundamentally conditioned by society. There are here no souls without bodies; and no individuals without the environment, direct or indirect, of other living wills.

Consider the duality of spirit and matter. Is the earthly circumstance of no account? Granted that social reform may mistakenly remove the needed challenge of hard environment and finally lay on us a curse of comfort, what of a hardship that is not a challenge to

character, but a threat against it? Granted that heroic
souls may overcome the fleshly or material obstacle (as
a flower may be seen forcing its way between concrete
slabs), what of those who cannot overcome? Lord
Shaftesbury said that some children are not born into
the world but damned into it. Jesus also had a trench-
ant word for those who place stumbling blocks against
the feet of "these little ones." The environment is but
the trellis on which the vines may climb, so we are
glibly told. Verily; but without the trellis the vines will
trail in dust. "The soul of reformation is the reformation of the soul," comes the platitude. True again; but
if some apostle Paul were here to-day to raise a congregation to a seventh heaven of spiritual fervor, and the
meeting were interrupted by some one closing doors
and windows and pumping carbonic acid gas into the
atmosphere, where then would be the spiritual fervor?
Where then would be the "reformation of the soul?"
There would be only a busy gasping for breath. It is
Jonathan Brierley's illustration. Nor is it pointless; for
there are physical environments and economic conditions on our planet which do stifle spiritual growth as
surely as, if less sensationally than, carbonic-acid gas
would kill a congregation.

That other duality, the essential linking of the individual with society, is not less momentous in its implications. We speak admiringly of the self-made man.
There is no such animal, and if there were he would be

so funny that there would be need to keep him in his own cage in some far corner of the zoo lest the other animals should laugh themselves to death. Our magazines are rife with accounts of the self-made man. Self-made? The first fact about him is that a mother went down to the gates of death that he might be born. He comes with all human history (and much of divine history) beating in his blood. Then he is fed on foods which other hands have harvested; wears clothes which other hands have woven; walks down streets which other men have built; is protected by laws which other men have drafted; uses language which many a "mute, inglorious Milton" has wrought until it rings like steel and shines like a cloth of gold; and breathes liberties which many a martyr has died to purchase. Yet he has the abysmal ignorance and the mountainous impudence to proclaim himself a "self-made man"! There is always something given to a man's hand, says Robert Louis Stevenson: "even if it be only four fingers and a thumb." Doctor Joseph Parker made the final retort to one who came and inflatedly described himself as a self-made man. "Sir," Doctor Parker answered—"Sir, you relieve the Lord of a great responsibility."

In our day, the interdependence of mankind is such that the ends of the world are at the end of every street. Recently it was discovered that the lack of orders in a New England textile-mill was due to the sudden failure of the market in a section of Korea.[2] Why had the market failed? Because in that section of Korea the main manufacture was hair-nets, and the American fashion of bobbed hair had brought the people to impoverishment. The world has shrunk to so small a neighborhood that when women bob their hair in America the falling hairpins hit a whole section in Korea (leaving it stunned) and then ricochet to stop the machinery in a New England textile mill. How amazing that in such a world Christian preaching should have been socialized of recent date and even then with hesitation! One greatly honored in the whole Church took issue with the contention that only recently had preaching become vigorously socialized.[3] He took exception to our modern narrowing of the adjective "prophetic"—as when we speak of "prophetic" preaching and mean the declaration of the social implicates of the Christian faith. He insisted that the prophets were first of all men with a sense of God, and that without that primary conviction their judgment on human oppression would have been robbed of purpose and power. His contention cannot be gainsaid. He insisted, further, that eighteenth-century evangelicalism instituted prison reforms and assailed the curse of slavery. Again, his plea was just. Yet it was that same evangelicalism which permitted a pious slave-trader, during a voyage when the ship's hold was full of negroes captured into slavery, to descend horrified on a group of his sailors gambling with dice on the deck on Sunday. He confiscated the tools of sin and threatened to make any man walk the plank who again desecrated God's Sabbath. Mr. Beard in *The Rise of American Civilization* is authority for that story; and there is that other, which Doctor Joseph Fort Newton relates,[4] of Sir John Bowring writing the hymn "In the Cross of Christ I glory" at the very time that he was engaged in the iniquitous opium war fought by the British in China. No generation has left the social gospel unproclaimed—and certainly not the eighteenth century—but it is yet true that only recently has the Church (and now only in certain sections) come to honest grips with the social demands of Jesus.

2

But did not Jesus content Himself with a message to the individual heart? Did He not refuse to entangle Himself with the secular movements of His day? Verily; but "individualistic" in the strict sense of that adjective will never do justice to the sweep and impact of His teaching. But was it not His method to leave us deathless principles? We doubt it. Principles are a figment until they shine in a face, just as ideals are void until they glow in a character. Jesus primarily did not teach principles: He bequeathed an eternal quality of life. He spoke dicta which will endure when heaven and earth have passed away; but His teaching came as often (perhaps more often) in stories or in concrete instances as in dicta. Had Jesus no word about a prevalent materialism? Did He not say to the rich man (whom we would call one of our "key citizens"), "Thou fool!" Had Jesus no word about the evils of divorce? And what of that day when, in His home town synagogue, He dealt ruthlessly with "one hundred per cent" patriotism: "There were many widows in Israel in the days of Elijah," but the prophet of God was sent to a widow of another land! . . . "and there were many lepers in Israel in the time of Elisha,"[5] but the only leper healed by the prophet was a Syrian! It is written that they were filled with wrath, and made as if to fling Him over a precipice. Would we say of that sermon that it dealt in abstract principles? What would happen to Jesus to-day if in our America He should say to us: "Pride yourselves that you are a chosen people; thank God you are not as other nations; clutter your days with things, and bedevil your minds with a ceaseless rush and grasping—and God will bestow His truth on some simpler nation that still has windows opening on the mysterious sky"? What would happen to Him? And we seem to remember that He said something about those who "devoured widows' houses"[6] and who for a pretense made long prayers; and that He made outright attack on the graft that could turn God's temple "into a den of robbers."[7] And we recall phrases like "whited sepulchres"[8] spoken against the leaders of the Church itself, and a charge that the Church was binding on men's shoulders burdens grievous to be borne.

Jesus warned His disciples that they would "be delivered up to councils"[9]—trade councils and ecclesiastical councils. Small fear that some of His modern interpreters will meet any such fate!

Need the case be further pleaded? Jesus said in that prayer that was offered in the shadow of the Cross: "For their sakes I sanctify myself."[10] "I sanctify myself" is a motto with its eyes turned inward—the quest of one intent on an individual holiness. "For their sakes" is a motto with its eyes turned outward—the resolve of those intent on building a kingdom. Jesus made of the twain one. The individual gospel and the social are not to be put asunder when Christ has joined them together: the individual gospel alone is a selfishness, and the social gospel alone is a tree without roots. Through our individual holiness, if it be Christlike, there will ever beat the insistent note of a social passion.

3

During the last war the nations spent roughly one hundred eighty-six billion dollars in direct money costs. The indirect money costs are more difficult to reckon. Reckoning three thousand dollars for each life (and that is not dear, is it?) and making allowance for the cost of industrial chaos, it has been estimated that the indirect money costs were about one hundred and fifty-two billion dollars more. We of America spent a paltry twenty-three billion dollars as our share,[11] but that was

enough to have paid all the expenses of our government
for one hundred and twenty years prior to the war's out-
break. This was the trivial end of the bill. There were
millions of desolated homes. There was the sowing of
the dragon's teeth of new wars. There were whole
peoples fed on a diet of mixed truth and lies miscalled
propaganda. There was hatred deliberately injected
into the veins of people normally humane. Heroism?
Yes, of a truth! An incredible and heartbreaking heroism before which we bow in reverence, as those
"bought with a price." But the worst indictment of war
is that it takes such heroism for a purpose of destruc-
tion when, harnessed to constructive tasks, it could
remake the world. Preparedness, we are told, will as-
sure peace. It never has! From the foundation of organ-
ized life peoples have prepared for war, but peace is still
far to seek. Certain of the warring nations in the last
great conflict were measurably prepared. Why did not
they escape the impact of war? "Ah," comes the retort,
"they lacked the will to peace." Then why do our mili-
tarists not tell us that preparedness is a curse if we lack
the will to peace? For the hundreds of thousands under
arms ready for war, how many thousands are assigned
under government funds to seek the causes of war and
to devise the machinery of peace? For all the millions
spent on war, what government has recently assigned
one million to promote international goodwill? Instead, there was in New York City on the Saturday of

Holy Week—the day between the day of the Cross and the day of the Open Tomb—a war parade, with hundreds of school children in the procession. We thought we saw Him on the sidewalk, watching. We wondered if He preferred His "funny little Cross." A preacher cannot be silent in face of this appalling curse. If he, the ambassador of Christ, is silent we should confess ourselves bankrupt both in brains and morals, and ask God to cleanse the planet of so wayward and cruel a race.

We are trying to indicate the need and the target of a socially minded message. War has been instanced. Industry would supply as urgent an illustration. Of that realm we need not despair. Industry, as we know it, is not much more than a hundred and forty years old. The discovery of steam-power, the invention of machines, and the factory system with its congestion of population are of comparatively recent date. Industry cannot suddenly be changed except at cost of chaos, but it should steadily be improved; for in so many regards it is an unfair threat against character. It is so monotonous in some of its processes that one wonders if it can breed any but monotonous folk—the light within their brains blown out. It denies to workers even the small privilege of ballot to help determine the conditions of their toil. It compels them to live under the menace of unemployment, so that to-day there are millions out of work in this Republic—a calamity directly affecting not less than one-fourth of the population of the richest nation in all history. Its gains are so unequally distributed that there are (without any exaggeration of language) the most glaring disparities of wealth and poverty, such that, if we had eyes to see, the residential area of any great city would appear as the flush on the cheek of a consumptive. To this impasse has the profit-motive in industry brought us! Should the preacher speak? One wonders, at times, if it is not too late. One hears the travailing multitudes saying to the Church, "Sleep on now and take your rest."[12] One hears an ominous rumbling, sees the gathering gloom, and fears the temple-veil of our social order may be rent in twain. Pray God it is not too late!

And (to cite another instance) what of our denomi-nationalism? That topic falls within the province of a socially minded ministry. Jesus spoke without fear or favor to the Church of His day, even while (had they allowed) He would have remained within it. There is a city of over one hundred thousand people with a con-siderable group of nominally Protestant Italians, some of whom are sprung from the Waldensian saints. Does any Church in that city minister to them? No, every Church is so busy raising its budget and maintaining its separate life, some of them in sections obviously overchurched, that this particular group goes unshep-herded. Can we suppose those Italians care much about the perpetuation of our denominational names, or the continuance of our sectional traditions? The particular church we serve has Germans, Italians, Scandinavians, and several hundred Czecho-Slavs in its membership. We can give assurance that they are mystified by the "five points" of recent theological debate, and know little and care less about the difference between an English Congregationalist and a Scotch Presbyterian.

Or, again, what of our prevalent materialism? For one hundred and twenty years we have been magnifying the body. As Bergson has said, most of our inventions have been extensions of the flesh. A telescope is a larger vision. A microscope is a keener eye. A telephone is a more powerful voice and ear. A gun is a longer arm and an explosive fist. A typewriter is a set of speedier and more skilful fingers. An automobile is a set of swift mechanical legs. An aeroplane is a bestowal of wings. This serving of the body we call "civilization," though in some of its aspects it is desperately uncivil.[13] We call it "progress." Why should we call it progress? It may be doom. Meanwhile life is whipped to an ever more insane tension and hurry. We are "always on the go." We are "going" at a speed without precedent. We do not know where we are going; and we dare not pause to find out, for if we pause we shall be counted "back numbers." But wherever we are going, whatever the goal of our civilization may be (and we must not stop to inquire, or we shall cease to be "live wires") —we are going! We must dig our tunnels, build our bridges, sell our merchandise, drive our myriad machines, fill our lives with furniture, and every now and again fight our wars. We *must*. Nobody knows why we must, but we must. Every real man must be "up and doing." But woe betide him if he should pause to ask which direction is "up," or what constitutes effective "doing." He is hopelessly impractical, if he pauses for questions so absurd. There have been other civilizations, almost as great as ours; and they are covered by desert-sand. There is no evidence that they brought deep joy even to their builders. It is treachery to suggest that our modern Tower of Babel is not worth the price of a shell-shocked soul. But let the saving treachery be spoken. Of a truth the Christian preacher will speak truth in face of modern war, modern denomination-alism, modern industry, modern materialism, not be-cause he is concerned primarily for conditions as such, but because, in the words of Jesus, they are binding on men and women and little children "burdens grievous to be borne." Who knows?—the heresy of the immedi-ate future (for which prophets are crucified) may not be theological: it may be economic and international.

4

If we have proved any case, there is a preaching to the social need, and it is an inescapable responsibility. But the question is, what shall be its mood and man-ner? The justifiable quarrel of many conservative-minded people in the Church is not against the validity of a social message, but against the inept and needlessly antagonizing way in which many preachers proclaim it. Quite obviously this preaching is beset with ambushes. There are men who indulge pious platitudes to the effect that if people would only follow Jesus war would be done away instanter. By the same token, that preacher also might be done away instanter. *How are* people to follow Jesus in industry? What are some of the guide-posts? People have a right to demand of the preacher clearer guidance than platitudes. Again, there are other preachers who rush in where experts fear to tread. Without any fund of authoritative knowledge they lay down in one sermon the "lines along which all the trains of industry shall run." There are still others who cite glaring but isolated instances of injustice as though they were general indictments; or who play the politician or the reformer, forsaking the higher station of the prophet. Admittedly the problems bristle; but that is no reason why the preaching of a social message should not be attempted; it is only a warning lest the task be botched. It is a fact beyond cavil that people, hearing a sermon of the social gospel, feel (and in frequent instances have a right to feel) that the hungry sheep "look up and are not fed." They suspect (nor is the suspicion altogether narrow-minded or ill-founded) that the preacher has forsaken the ambassadorship of Christ for the hustings of the agitator. How shall the social gospel be preached? How can the preaching of the social aspect of the one indivisible gospel be made effective?

Perhaps there will arise within the Church a new order of preachers the genius of whose message is its social passion. Some such are in the Church already; perhaps they should be released for a wider and itinerant ministry. But this would be no final answer to the question. The preacher must himself be the shepherd of his own flock. Every minister can become, within limits, an authority on some aspect of the social need. The books are available, and life under the curse is at his elbow to study. Often a simple statement of fact, without tirade or denunciation, would be in itself a powerful incentive. Do we tell our hearers that some nations, which we consider "backward nations," have established systems of unemployment-insurance and government "old age pensions"? Do we recite the easily accessible figures about the distribution of wealth in America? Have we quoted the army and navy estimates for the current year and compared them in amount with the money asked for foreign missions? The setting forth of these facts, without any berating of the congregation (which berating is always foolish), will not be in vain.

Certainly the Church, at whatever risk of loss in membership, must be made an inclusive fellowship. The compassing of that end, even if no direct mention were ever made of social needs, would be in itself an allaying of social bitterness glorious to behold. There is no other inclusive fellowship. A labor union or an employers' association is not inclusive: each in its own camp caters to those who make common cause in economic theory. A fraternal order is not inclusive: its ritual is secret. A luncheon club is not inclusive: its mind is notoriously standardized. A school is not inclusive: it sets limits of age. Most churches are not inclusive: they minister, perhaps of necessity, to a group— university, suburban, or artisan. But of all institutions the Church alone has chance to become inclusive, for only the Church builds on the common denominator of human life—on the sense of God. Nor will men honor the brotherhood until they recognize that Fatherhood which makes us one family. City churches especially have a great gift to bestow if they so order their life that, in a sacred place beyond the bitterness of class and racial strife, men can kneel together to pray "*Our* Father."

Series of sermons on the social aspect of the gospel are profitable. Yet they give appearance of a cleft in a gospel which is for the whole of life; and a series on "The Sins of the Industrial Order" might brand the minister as a propagandist, and antagonize a congregation. Denunciation may be in place if it is almost irresistibly impelled by a love for needy and suffering folk, but denunciation is usually a clumsy tool. In denunciation one flashing thrust cuts deeper than prolonged castigation. Many men in our Churches may be laboring better than we know for a more friendly social scheme. We were humbled the other day by a banker in our church who told us (not in any self-justification, but simply as a matter of interest) that he had spent the greater part of a year trying to devise a plan whereby in his complex business the employees could share both in profits and management, but that he had been driven (both by the inherent difficulty of the problem, and by the fact of a diverse mind in the system in which he was involved) to the recourse of a generous bonus and to the reluctant admission that such a plan as he desired was for the present beyond his best wisdom.

5

It is probably true that two rules hold good for "social" preaching. First, it should be tender appeal or ringing challenge to the individual rather than a thunderbolt aimed at large or at some broad territory of public oppression. An appeal to the individual! An appeal that men shall try to pay their social debt! The individuals to whom we preach are not "self-made" people: they are drowned debtors to a vast fund of human cheer, toil, and courage. An appeal that men shall not shirk social responsibility! For individuals as individuals are ultimately responsible for social ills. Strange how there is something wrong with the war-system and nothing wrong with individual angers and greeds! Strange how the glaring defect is always in the marriage custom and never in married people! Strange how when people go hungry the fault is in national distribution, and never in the selfishness of people like ourselves! Strange that militarism should be a baleful cloud mysteriously descending on us, and never the trampling instinct in your life and mine! Our preaching must press home the debt of the individual to the community, and the obligation of the individual to serve the community if he would fulfil the Christian "way." What is it to be a Christian? To accept the "cup of salvation"? To cultivate the walled garden of the soul? Yes. But that is not all: to be a Christian is to take up one's own cross. Not merely one's burden; we are conscripted to carry burdens: there is no escaping them. But we volunteer to carry crosses.[14] Crosses are other people's burdens—the shame of our city streets, the oppressions of industry, the loneliness of the immigrant, the guilt of the imprisoned, the pangs of the unemployed, and the sorrows of war. A man, if he would be a Christian, must carry his cross. Preaching to the social need is at best a wise, urgent, tender plea—specific in tone and import—addressed to the individual.

And is this the second rule that holds for the preaching of the social gospel?—the preacher shall again and again rigorously examine his own motives that his message may issue from a consciousness of God, a devo-

tion to Jesus, and a love of all mankind. That consciousness will save him from becoming partisan—and partisanship is a pitfall at the edge of every sermon. It is
easy to be partisan, the enthusiast of an "ism." It is
easy to pour paraffin of words on the flame of one's
own anger to watch how fiercely it can burn. It is easy
to become a propagandist of earth, as though the gospel
had no cosmic sweep. Labor agitation is not yet a fount
of pure wisdom. Sometimes that agitation has no better
counsel than that the poor shall seize the wealth that to
the wealthy has brought no joy; and sometimes it
covets the gains of Christian teaching without much desire to share its spirit. The consciousness of God, fealty
to Christ, and love of all mankind will save the
preacher likewise from dilution and disproportion in
his message. If the New Testament account of the
temptation of Jesus is His dramatization of a desperate
inner testing (a testing the more desperate because He
hungered only for the coming of the Kingdom of
God), must we not recognize that there Jesus confronted the alternative of a social crusade on the one
hand and, on the other, the revealing of God?—and
that His victory, though at cost of a Cross, was in choosing to be the revealer of God rather than the leader
of a national or economic crusade? "Social service"
must remain a truncated endeavor, ever drained by the
ebbing of its zeal, until it makes terms with the fact
that Jesus (the one Benefactor) spent whole nights in

prayer. His best gift was not bread or bodily healing.
In a world bereft of His Spirit the bread of a just economic order would become ashes, and health of body
with continuance of days would be no blessing that we
should desire it. His best gift to the world was Himself! Must we not say that our best gift as preachers
(though to say it is conviction of sin) is—ourselves?
Nay, not ourselves; rather ourselves overcome and lost
in Christ! He is Lord also of the "social gospel." The
social gospel is the woe of the world upon His heart
and ours—His burden and His dream become articulate through us.

This gospel must be preached in such fearlessness
that we also may "be delivered up to councils." People
will be hostile: the servant is not above his Lord. They
may be justifiably hostile: the preaching may impress
them as being of men rather than of God, as reflecting
a partisan reading of events rather than the rigor and
persuasiveness of Christ—in which event our road is
the old road of prayer and confession, back to God. But
people may be hostile because the preaching is true and
unpalatable—in which event our road is the old road
of the Cross!

The social gospel must be preached in fearlessness,
but it must be gathered back into the disclosure of God
in Christ. People will at last be won by His sufferings
who will never be won by socialism, republicanism,
state capitalism or "normalcy."

Let the preacher preach the social gospel. If he shirk
that task, he may escape discomfort, but he will not escape himself or Christ. Let him preach a truer nation-
alism. Let him preach a fairer industry—whose smoke
becomes the pattern of His Face against the sky. Let
him cleanse the temple. Let him overturn by his zeal
the tables of the money changers. But let him keep that
preaching ever in the constraint of Christ's love; lest,
wandering into propagandist realms, it is slain. Let him
so preach that in all things "He may be exalted."

CHAPTER FIVE

PREACHING CHRIST TO THE INDIVIDUAL OF TO-DAY

CHAPTER FIVE

PREACHING CHRIST TO THE INDIVIDUAL
OF TO-DAY

THE SOCIAL GOSPEL,
so-called, and the individual gospel are not two: they
are the terms of one paradox. It has been written: "If
religion ends with the individual, it ends."[1] Verily. But
if it does not begin with the individual, it never begins,
and has no being. The seed of all things human is self-
hood. Personality is the pole around which the elec-
trons of the social life revolve. Granted that we are
"bound in the bundle of life" more closely than leaves
are bound in the life of a tree, each leaf is yet different
and distinct. If mankind is a stupendous organism, personalities are yet its life-giving cells. The individual is
still the fount and nexus of our social life.

If this prime fact is forgotten we shall be found
speaking of movements and causes as if they were not
composed of people. Let human solidarity be proclaimed: *one* man must proclaim it; and, before he can
proclaim it, *one* mind must vision it—yea, and vision it
by standing apart from the multitudinous world. Every

crusade comes to its spear-point in one consecrated spirit. Enthusiasm may seem as undifferentiated as a wave; actually it is the contagion of a good courage leaping from character to character. "The spirit of the Lord came upon Gideon,"[2] says the old story. Literally the words are: "The Spirit of the Lord put on Gideon —clothed Himself with Gideon." The brooding of the Eternal invaded society through a chosen personality. It is the immemorial way! "And a man shall be . . . as the shade of a great rock."[3] So easily we forget,

> It takes a soul,
> To move a body; it takes a high-souled man,
> To move the masses, even to a cleaner stye;
> It takes the ideal, to blow a hair's-breadth off
> The dust of the actual.—Ah, your Fouriers failed,
> Because not poet enough to understand
> That life develops from the within.[4]

It takes not only a high-souled man to move the masses, but, since the masses also are men, it takes the co-operation of all human units in the mass. Every cause and movement must finally come as suppliant to an individual altar.

It has been our contention in these chapters that the method and mind of Jesus are regulative for Christian preaching. Behold, then, His reverence for the person. He did not seek the crowd; He sought the individual, and the crowd sought Him. He began His ministry, not by clamoring at the gates of civil power or by challenging the Temple, but by laying siege to the hearts of the two obscure men on a country road.)Then He chose twelve average men "that they might be with him."[5] His aim was not to give millions a whitewash of religion, but to make twelve men alive with it. On them He lavished the wealth of His gospel. They were average, as their compatriots well knew: "Hath any of the rulers believed on him?"[6] The question was its own answer. The disciples were drawn from "Main Street." They quarrelled. They were not very brave. Often they were childish in their thinking. Yet Jesus made them immensely useful: it is possible that they have more influence in any city to-day than any twelve men now living there whom we might name. They were twelve men, not twelve copies. None of them reminds us of any other. Philip looks before he leaps; Peter leaps before he looks. Thomas was a sceptic to the last, but Jesus chose him and kept him as one of the inner circle—a fact worth noticing! James and John were nicknamed "sons of thunder," perhaps because, like their native hills, they were capable of sudden storms. Yet they were average men. It would appear that Jesus could find scores like them in every congregation. And —this is the mightily significant fact—whereas He might have headed a social crusade, He chose to give Himself with apparent wastefulness to twelve obscure individuals.

I

No man can preach to the individual who does not go where he lives, and who does not say to him in urgent fidelity of pastoral care, "Would that my soul were in your soul's stead!"[7] There are ministers who decry "the futility of ringing doorbells." Some of us understand the force of that caption. We know how the minister's burden of administration has increased. We know how elusive is the average parishioner—exiled from his home by the rush and distraction of modern life. We know that it does not appear heroic to leave calling-cards at unresponsive doors, or in the hands of apartment-house doormen—though in New York that latter is no coward's task, our doormen being more impressive than Napoleon and more arbitrary than Jove. But we know also, from actual experience, that a card left in a man's home one day may the next bring that man to his minister to seek counsel or to give release to a pent-up soul. Those who speak of the futility of ringing doorbells do not tell us how a friendship can be built on fifteen-minute interviews given in an apparent parsimony of time; nor do they provide an alternative method for winning such confidence as the friendliness of a home undoubtedly inspires. Jesus apparently spent much of His time going into people's homes. Some of us, however perplexed with the difficulties, cannot find any substitute for that pastoral care.

Our mutual ignorance is so appalling that we need not add to it by artificial barriers. Each of us is imprisoned behind walls of flesh. We do not see the other man: we see, or think we see, a spirit looking out through two little windows called eyes. We do not hear the other man: we interpret the tapping of a Morse code on the tympanum of our ear. What with the clumsiness of the Morse code and the dullness of the interpretation we know pitiably little of what is happening in our neighbor's hermitage of bone and sinew.

> God pity all the brave who go
> The common way, and wear
> No ribboned medal on their breasts,
> No laurels in their hair.
>
> God pity all the lonely folk
> With griefs they do not tell,
> Women waking in the night,
> And men dissembling well.
>
> And who but God shall pity them
> Who go so quietly,
> And smile upon us when we meet,
> And greet us pleasantly?[8]

Organization in the church can quickly usurp the place and time better given to a pastoral ministry. There is a story of the factory that installed a new filing-system so marvellous and complete that business had to be suspended to keep the filing-system in work-

ing trim. Many a church suspends its real business in
zeal for an organization. It runs printer's ink instead of
red blood, and brings forth programmes instead of
souls imbued with the Eternal. Nor is this an easy gibe:
the danger is real. The minister who knows the books
on his shelves better than the fleshly volumes in his parish will not for long preach with authority. The best
sermon is that preached in such human understanding
that a hearer can say: "It was preached for me as
though I had been alone."

The preacher may be appraised, as may any other
man, by this simple but final test: "Does he see faces or
things?" There are business men who see only things—
sales-resistance, charts, profits; there are other business
men who see faces—the faces of those who work for
them, and the faces of those who have no work. There
are statesmen who see only things—battleships, voting-
booths, newspaper-headlines; and there are other statesmen who see faces—faces of the poor, faces of little
children, and myriad faces slain in war. There are
would-be preachers who see only things—church buildings, card-indices, year-book figures; and there are other
preachers, ordained by a tenderness beyond the hand of
man, who see faces—faces wistful and sin-scarred,
lonely and brave. Jesus saw nothing on earth but faces;
nothing in heaven but faces; nothing in hell but faces.
Always He swung the conversation back to the human.
If men discussed the prospect of harvest, He would say:

"See the fields of faces white already unto harvest."[9] If men were absorbed in the little quest for things, he summoned them to a nobler crusade: "Come ye after me, and I will make you fishers of men."[10] He lays His hands on all our institutions—the church, the factory, the prison, and the school—and asks: "What is its human issue?"

Elisha, so the old story goes, thought he could awaken by proxy a certain dead child. He imagined that his staff carried in the hands of his servant, Gehazi, would bestow the life-giving virtue. But Gehazi returned and told him, "The child is not awaked."[11] Not until Elisha was himself stretched out on the lifeless form, lips against lips, eyes against eyes, hands against hands, did the cold flesh become warm with new life. Therein is a parable of pastoral care. The staff-method (even though the staff be the largest organization or the strongest letter-file) is impotent to quicken life from death: that miracle comes only as warmth goes out of a man and life is laid on life in sacrificial nearness.

2

The individual in our day is a new man. Psychology has revealed in him unsuspected depths and mysteries. Our visible days and deeds, we now know, are in relation to the subconscious self as a lighted ocean liner to the dark sea on which it sails. We dance in the gay saloon, and imagine meanwhile that our little lighted world is the only world. But when we walk the decks we become aware of a heaving ocean. Lights flicker: are they mainland or another ship? Away stretches that ocean toward continents of mystery and islands of the unknown! So we walk the decks of our conscious self and become aware of a hidden universe all unexplored. The lilt of an old song can quicken memories of long ago: where have those memories been stored? The command is given to a hypnotized woman (and this incident is actual): "After you wake you will carry a book from that table, and put it on the bookshelf."[12] She wakes and obeys. Asked why she has moved the book from the table to the shelf, she says: "I do not like to see things untidy; the shelf is the place for books." That is not the real reason. Yet she thought it the real reason. Do we often give ourselves and other people a false account of the motives that sway us—ourselves not knowing they are false? The subconscious, it appears, is not a series of cupboards in which memories and re-solves are stored: it is a living organism with its own processes, more amazing perchance than those which comprise the world of matter.

Psychologists have left the impression that the sub-conscious is the realm of the devious and the unworthy, but why should it not be also (and more deeply) the secret place of angels? In our boyhood we once saw miners lined up at the pit-head after a colliery explo-

sion. They were almost fighting for the chance to attempt the rescue of their comrades from that fume-
filled darkness. They had trudged commonplace
through commonplace days until that day: where had
that heroism been lurking? The dull filament of their
nature glowed then, and with unearthly fire: where
was the fire kindled? Emerson once said: "I like my
poems best, because I did not write them." Who *did*
write them? There is a so much deeper and vaster
world within us than we have dreamed.

Mr. Lippmann has written concerning the modern
man: "He is one man to-day and another to-morrow,
one person here and another there."[13] The statement is
mild indeed. The modern man is a hundred different
people at every moment in every place.

> Where is one that, born of woman, altogether can escape
> From the lower world within him, moods of tiger and
>   of ape?[14]

asks Tennyson. The answer is, "Nobody." There is a
mood of tiger in us—a snarling anger. There is a mood
of ape—a senseless copying of our neighbors. If we
wished to be cynical we might continue the zoological
list and say that there is a mood of sheep within us—a
cowardly scurrying with the mob, and a mood of mule
—a most stubborn cussedness; a menagerie of moods
with days when the whole menagerie is in an uproar.
But if we wished to be true we would continue the list

still further, and say there is a hero in us, a philosopher, a dreamer and a saint. There is a mood of André, of Socrates, of Milton and of Gandhi.

> Where is he that, born of woman, altogether can escape
> From the *higher* world within him?

The only undiscovered country is the country of the soul. We have learned in these latter days how vast is that land—how dark with jungles and marshes, how glorious with sunrise and mountain-height.

Yet, by some strange contradiction, our civilization forbids man to explore this universe of self-hood so recently disclosed, but compels him by its curse of externalism to live on the surface of his days. Noises fierce and frantic assault him—noises of street and factory when he works, and the radio's spluttering banalities when he is at home. Advertising assaults his eyes, and fairly shrieks at him begging him to buy. Doctor Halford E. Luccock has quoted figures[15] to show that whereas the average man of a hundred years ago had seventy-two wants of which sixteen might be called necessities, the man of to-day has acquired four hundred and eighty-four wants of which ninety-four might be called necessities; and that there are sold in the United States to-day three hundred and sixty-five thousand different articles—a thousand, it will be noticed, for each day in the year. Furthermore this victimized individual of to-day has "movies" for his daily diet; and "movies"

are produced to make money, and are likely therefore
to appeal to the primitive emotions by methods bereft
of authentic art or insight. The newspapers are his daily
reading—and how many newspapers are edifying? By
an oft-quoted definition it is not news if a dog bites a
man, but it is news if a man bites a dog. Most newspapers build their subject matter on that definition, despite the fact that it is untrue. It *is* news when a dog
bites a man (especially if we know the dog and the
man), for of such small vicissitudes the fabric of our
days is woven. It is *not* news when a man bites a dog:
it is a case for the psychopathic ward on which people
of worth will not feed their minds. Some of our newspapers read like bulletins from the psychopathic ward.
The movies, the advertising, the newspapers (with
some shining exceptions) create a standardized mind
inconspicuous for its depth.

> Should banded unions persecute
>   Opinion, and induce a time
>   When single thought is civil crime
> And individual freedom mute,[16]

a poet dolefully sang, and threatened to seek exile in
some tropic isle if that "time" should ever come:

> Yet waft me from the harbour-mouth,
>   Wild wind! I seek a warmer sky,
>   And I will see before I die
> The palms and temples of the South.[16]

Had he lived now and sought that exile he would probably have found the "temples of the South" covered with cigarette advertising of impeccable veracity; and under the palms a machine to climb the trees, pluck the dates, pit them, and pack them in standardized boxes at so many hundred boxes per minute.

The forces of our day "persecute opinion" and make "single thought" a crime with greater severity than any banded union. The machine has come to complete the regimentation of the modern mind. Men used at least to be "hands": now they are interchangeable parts to be thrown on the scrap-heap as soon as they are outworn. Mr. Lippmann says again: "There is something radically new in the modern world . . . this new thing is . . . power-driven machinery."[17] Mr. James Truslow Adams, Mr. Arthur Pound,[18] and Mr. John Herman Randall, Jr., have tried to predict the world that will result from "this new thing"; but they admit that the portent is so epochal that they cannot prophesy what transformations it will work. Mr. Randall writes: "It was far easier for the man of the fourteenth century to foresee our own bustling civilization than for us to behold the new world that is coming to pass."[19] Already the city has become supreme, industrial control has been rapidly (and some would say, ominously) unified, the gigantic hand of business has been laid upon our civic and national policies, mass production has almost slain craftsmanship, monotony of toil has dulled the mind and provoked a thirst for cheap and lurid pleasures, individual liberties have been curtailed, and new social groupings have suddenly sprung from the limbo of the unimagined. For the preacher in his concern for the individual the main factor is the dulling of man's finer sensibilities by a machine-age, and the thwarting of his distinctive gifts and character. The individual of to-day is living not merely in a new climate but in a new geological age.

It is a coincidence, perhaps ironic, perhaps providential, that at the moment when psychology has uncovered the depths of selfhood, civilization should condemn us to the shallows of a fragmentary, harassed, and machine-driven existence. In that clash of interests human nature remains the same in its elemental hopes and fears. Mr. Lippmann apparently believes that the machine has changed the very constitution of man's being; but, in actuality, it has only temporarily crushed him. Some of us hold the faith that human nature will rebel at no distant time against the dominance of the machine, which man himself has made and which man himself will yet learn to control. The Frankenstein monster is, after all, like his smaller brethren the robots, fiction rather than history. Man will not long endure the shackles of standardizing forces; he will relegate the machine to its alloted hours, and return to the creative joy of craftsmanship. Meanwhile these forces are upon us. They have shaped and will shape the individual. They must shape the preacher's message, dictate a new mood, and give to the Eternal Gospel a new accent and urgency.

3

We inquire, therefore, for the marks of such preaching as our age requires and the immemorial needs of human life exact. It must be pungent preaching, pictorial in the best sense of the word, direct in its friendliness; eschewing both the ornamentation which conceals the truth and the "grand manner" which has made the pulpit a laughing-stock. So much is patently clear. But our immediate inquiry concerns not the technique of the musician, but rather the motifs of his music. What should be the dominant themes of preaching in our day?

It should exalt man's individual worth. In an age when secular pressure reduces him to a digit and almost to a cipher, when a cynical fiction portrays him as a fleshly parcel of meannesses and fears, the pulpit must trace the gold within his clay and recall him to his rightful destiny. Of late everything has conspired to rob a man of himself. The war made him a number on a metal disc, and used him as a human bullet. The new astronomy lifted up our planet as a "very little thing," as a speck of cosmic dust, and made man the speck of a speck. The new evolutionary science traced our span of life as a tiny shadow of dim-stretching time, and made man the shadow of a shadow. The new factory system made him the tappet-rod of a machine. Let it be said of the preacher: "He, at least, believed in soul, was very sure of God." Perhaps the pulpit of the coming day must be consecrated to the task of vindicating the soul against the machine, as the pulpit of the last generation vindicated it against the vastnesses of time and space.

Jesus told His twelve friends that they were the "light of the world," though they seemed but candles flickering in the smoke of their prejudice. He told them they were so precious in the sight of heaven, that God would search His planet-cottage with unwearying scrutiny should they ever be lost. He told them that whenever they turned their faces to the Ideal Life joy flooded every inlet of the skies: "there shall be joy in heaven."[20] That message remains. Man is a paradox of dust and divinity, and no paradox can ever be resolved into one of its terms. If man is stigmatized as earthy, that branding comes of man's own mind, which must have converse with heaven before it can condemn anything as being of earth. "Man may be base," said Emerson; "but how do we know that he is base?" Man cannot be scorned as little except under the brooding of some vastness; and if Mr. Lippmann sees a discord in modern life it is because of some prior harmony set in his own soul. In a European museum there is a brick from ancient Babylon, and on it the print of a dog's foot set there while the clay was still plastic. But beneath the print of the dog's foot, and going deeper, is the print of the king's seal!

There is a royal needs-must in man's nature. It may have come by devious ways through tribal customs and old wives' gossip; even so, that would constitute no threat against its validity. Everything else has come by devious ways—medicine by way of the fakir and psychology by way of the teller of dreams; and to trace an origin is not to resolve a mystery. This "ought" may speak with varying witness—the old religious rite of widow-burning in India is considered murder in the United States—but that variation cannot render it invalid. Science also speaks with varying accent—the diagnosis given by the medicine-man in India being startlingly different from the diagnosis given by the Mayo clinic. Yet the truth of science remains one truth, and the truth of conscience remains one truth. There is an "ought" in man's nature. There is a hidden loveliness. There is a sky of compassion arching his fussy little charities. Nor can the jaundiced gloom of our contemporary pessimists ever cancel the splendor that lined the hemlock-cup of Socrates. Milton remains with all the grand diapasons of his organ soul; and Lincoln abides, so that in his gaunt homeliness against the darkness of the Civil War, we seem to hear him say:

> O Beauty on the darkness hurled,
> Be it through me you shame the world.[21]

Such spirits do shame the world—and save it. There is no gulf fixed between them and our average humanity. Their victory is the earnest of the triumph which their lowliest brethren are ordained to win. In a machine age the preacher can hear mankind still say:

> I cannot chain my soul; it will not rest
> In its clay prison, this most narrow sphere;
> It has strange impulse, tendency, desire,
> Which nowise I account for nor explain,
> But cannot stifle. . . .[22]

Let the preacher trace that "impulse, tendency, desire" back to its home in God who makes men for Himself. Such preaching shall not be in vain: the soul, listening, shall stand at salute knowing that truth is passing down the lines.

Preaching to-day must sound the note of moral earnestness. In the old Methodism there were preached "black sermons," so-called; and black they were! They pulled on human fears as a man might pull on the rope of a funeral bell. They pictured the penalties of hell with such vividness that the flames started in the eyes of the congregation. There was some truth in that preaching (for Jesus did not altogether disavow the appeal to fear), but there was more of error, for it was alien to His dominant mood and method. We cannot wish the return of "black sermons," but we might well wish the return of the overwhelming urgency that

shook those sermons like a passion, and which compelled a preacher to say in that time: "My friends, I
have cleared myself this day of your blood."

Standards shift, but the soul's decree, of which our
changing standards are but "broken lights," is not
moved; and the man who tries to move it is visited by
terrors. Standards must change. The Victorian code is
not identical with the Moral Law. The Victorians
treated sins of the flesh as doubly black, while sins of
temper they painted light gray, regarding them as defects rather than sins; and this despite the fact that
Jesus, while He assuredly had no condonation for sins
of the flesh, yet spoke with sharper condemnation to
the churchly Pharisees than to Mary Magdalene. The
Victorian tradition was fusty and unbalanced, yet it is
doubtful if our casual and flippant "freedom" improves
upon it. In superior tones we deprecate the conventions
of the "nineties" as a "defence" against life, an "escape"
from the facts; and such they were. Yet Victorian restraints made noble literature and art; they issued in
great discoveries in geography and science. Perhaps
creativeness is never found except as the outbreaking on
a high level of a life-spirit that is saved from over-in-
dulgence on a fleshly level. Admit the Victorian conventions to be a "defence": is our modern flippancy
aught else? When people are at pains to show how free
they are, we may be quite sure that they have wounded
life deeply and dare not admit the hurt. For the mod-

ern libertine to deny authority because the outward authorities have seemed to crumble is a sardonic thing of tragic texture. He says there is no Ark of God; but his fever-ridden eyes make known an Ark within—yea, make known that he, like Uzzah of old, has set impious hands upon the Ark and has been struck dead even while he lives. The day for "black sermons" has not entirely gone.

Ask an honest man in the pew what he requires of his preacher, and he will admit ere long that he has scant respect for a pulpit that does not make the pews uncomfortable. People are driven from the church not so much by stern truth that makes them uneasy as by weak nothings that make them contemptuous. If we fail to preach sin and its redemption, the novelists and dramatists will become worthier ambassadors in our stead. Some Shakespeare will paint the darkness of remorse:

> Canst thou not minister to a mind diseased,
> Pluck from the memory a rooted sorrow?[23]

and some Masefield sing the gladness of conversion:

> I did not think, I did not strive,
> The deep peace burnt my me alive;
> The bolted door had broken in,
> I knew that I had done with sin.
> I knew that Christ had given me birth
> To brother all the souls on earth.[24]

The note of moral earnestness is the more needed when conduct and thought have become standardized. Who is responsible for Tammany graft? Everybody, and therefore nobody! Conscience is spread so thin over our modern multitudes that it disappears. The old cartoon showed a circle of men responsible for Tammany graft—every man walking in the circle single-file and every man pointing an accusing thumb at the man behind. We will not steal from our neighbor, but we are not so scrupulous with the income-tax report. In that latter instance conscience escapes in the complexity of life; it runs out through remote and multitudinous agents until it is lost. Who is to blame for the tabloid press? Not the editor solely: he is no longer his own voice as in an earlier day of journalism, but the mouthpiece of a syndicate; and the paper is now a gigantic business venture. Advertisers are involved: must not their wishes be respected when the policy of the paper is in question? A host of workers are involved—people whose livelihood rests upon that publication: surely their interests should be consulted. The vast army of readers is involved: they should not be given what they want (despite the journalist's frequent plea; for, on that argument, we should cut a man's throat if he wants us to do it), but their desire cannot be flouted if journalism is to endure. Who is to blame? Everybody—and therefore nobody. Clearly our day needs a new and more rigorous concept of duty—such a concept as will forbid an editor to sell himself to a combine, or an advertiser to attempt to interfere with truth, or a workman to make a living by the dissemination of scandal, or a reader to patronize a journal that cheapens public taste. Ultimately public responsibility becomes private obligation; and a voice sounds: "Thou art the man." The modern pulpit must be that voice—not in scolding, but in kindliness; yet not in compromise, but with unflinching truth. The pulpit must be a conscience, winsome yet true, to each succeeding age; as Jesus is a living Conscience "alway, unto the end of the age."

In every generation great preaching has lived in a mood of compassion, nor is that mood less needed in a regimented era. The Evangelists do not use the word translated in our Bible "compassion" except of Jesus or in the record of His parables. It is *His* word: He yearned over people with a love and longing that were pain. That compassion has found fine expression in the lines of Frederic W. H. Myers:

> Only like souls I see the folk thereunder,
>   Bound who should conquer, slaves who should be
>   kings,—
> Hearing their one hope with an empty wonder,
>   Sadly contented in a show of things;—
>
> Then with a rush the intolerable craving
>   Shivers throughout me like a trumpet call,—
> Oh to save these! to perish for their saving,
>   Die for their life, be offered for them all![25]

Oscar Wilde once remarked that there is enough suffering in any London lane to show that God does not love men. He revised that opinion when he himself reached the place of suffering and found it the place of a Presence. Yet the preacher whose imagination is quick will find enough suffering in any congregation to leave him awestruck. He will yearn over his people with something of that compassion that was in Jesus. He will perhaps have the strange imagining of everybody in his church coming down the aisle to cast his burden on the chancel in front of a cross—the man of bitter memory forever excavating his own heart, the mother who has recently stood by an open grave, the father out of work, the employer sorrowful because there seems no alternative but to throw men out of work, the young woman for whom circumstance has closed the door of her talent and who must now be content with a second-best endeavor, and the elderly man who to-morrow must lie on an operating-table. Down that aisle they come, showing of what courageous stuff our humanity is made, piling up their burdens on the chancel floor until the black heap lifts the roof and makes its own entreaty to the sky. If the preacher has not been visited by some such imagining it were better for him that he should not preach!

Nor has our inventive civilization banished that woe. If Jesus saw people in His day harassed and distracted "as sheep not having a shepherd," does He look with a less pitying eye on our city crowds? Electricity can work wonders, but it cannot light the pathway to peace. Our machines can generate stupendous power, but not power to renew a diseased will. Our elevators whisk up sixty, seventy, eighty floors; but they cannot lift us nearer God. Our wealth is fabulous, but it cannot buy back our childhood prayers. Beneath the crackling brilliance of American success there lives a pathetic wistfulness. The treasure-chest of the world has become a box of vanities. The defences of a world—its money, its titles, its amenities—are a matchwood wall when sorrow comes in like a flood. Nor can the gerrymandering of psychological cults or the arid comfort of humanism provide any lasting resource.

Like a pilgrim of old bound for the Holy Land, he takes his staff and goes, but not in anger or contempt, rather in bewilderment and in discontent with himself, oppressed by a shallow breathing and a sultry air.[26]

So Henry Dwight Sedgwick writes concerning the disillusionment that makes the recluse. The words bid fair to become the description of many a modern soul. Meanwhile the only Holy Land is the fact of Christ and the saving mystery of His cross. "Be kind," Ian Maclaren was wont to say; "be kind: every man you meet is fighting a hard battle."[27] That kindness is an authentic note for modern preaching.

So also is the note of cheer and challenge. The gospel is not an easy optimism, yet it gives sure promise of re-

demption. Those who make confession to God and
restitution to men and trust Him for strength find the
tides of a life-giving Spirit flooding into the little pool
of their mortal days to give an ocean fulness. Great
preaching is always a *sursum corda*. Men will not be
satisfied with a diagnosis of their present ills: they crave
some pledge of vitality. The picture of themselves as
they are will not finally content them: they would fain
see the "photograph of themselves that God keeps in
heaven to save Him from despair."[28] "Sursum corda,"
the preacher cries. He tells men that if the waters of
life are bitter with the acid of sorrow or sin, Christ can
generate there an electric contagion of new character
that will break the acid waters into the hydrogen of
peace and the oxygen of power. If the preacher has cast
himself on Christ in scorn of consequence that telling
will evidence its own verity.

With the cheer must come the challenge. Read the
world of business closely: you will find that it is shame-
faced if it does not discover its adventure. The Grand
Central Terminal becomes a crown of jewelled lights
against the darkness. "Good advertising," the cynic
replies. Yes; but more: the supposedly drab world of
business eager to "catch the threads of vanishing
dreams," the flair of the poet and adventurer coming
to its own! There was in New York recently an exhibi-
tion of engineers' models, every one of them the work
of some amateur engineer; of business men whom

money-making did not content, whose creativeness and craftsmanship must find an outlet. Preaching must indicate an outlet for a new creativeness. It must say to the business man concerning a new social order: "I cannot do it. But you—with your skill and courage—you can do it. It will cost you suffering, but through the suffering you may have a prophet's joy and lead mankind from an industrial wilderness to a promised land." No real boy would wish to play football if it did not carry some risk and danger, and no real man or woman thrills to an easy life. Recently a doctor treated for a severe head-cold one of Admiral Byrd's staff. That man had gone through the whole antarctic year without a cold (temperatures far below zero are not hospitable to strepticoccus germs!), but when he returned to civilization he fell victim to sickness. Therein is a parable: the soul of man is never so healthy as in some dangerous outpost of the human advance. Let preaching sound its challenge. Let it strike the Garibaldi note: red-shirts will not be lacking! Let it say with Christ: "If any man would come after Me let him take up his cross daily—and follow!"[29]

But the preacher's best endeavor will be the mediation of a Presence. The whole duty of preaching in any age, and especially in our age infested by noise and ravaged by externals, is the bequeathing of the sense of God. It is an irony that in this raucous day, when men and women are hungry for preaching that will breathe

a stillness on their spirits, churches should try to com-
pete with the clamor of the street. It has been said of
George Frederick Watts that whenever he was touched
by a sunset or a friendship his face would appear "as
though a flame had been lighted." The world covets
preaching that will be true to that description. George
Borrow wandered into the fields of Wales and fell into
conversation with a group of gypsies.[30] He did not talk
to them of religion, yet all unknowingly the virtue
went out of him; so that when he made as if to go they
besought him, saying: "Oh, it was kind of you to come
. . . that you might bring us God." He made it clear
that he was neither priest nor minister, but they en-
treated him the more: "Oh, sir, do give us God." Such
is the agelong cry that the world lifts to its pulpits:
"Oh, sir, do give us God." If the preacher has kept the
white vigil of prayer, if he has made friends with the
silence in which God speaks, that cry will be his joy;
if not, it will be his inward doom. The preacher's best
offering is the gift of God. For *that* men will still raise
hungry hands even when our best social schemes have
found fulfilment, even when prison-yards are gone,
even when there is bread and to spare, even when
tenements have yielded place to gardens. *That* is the
deepest benefaction: "Oh, sir, give us God." Christ lived
upon a cross and died upon it that He might give men
—God. In Him a world of mystery and light descended
upon earth's sordid days and made them radiant.

To mediate the Presence—that is at once the preacher's burden, his sovereign gift, his sufficient credential, his enduring joy: "It was kind of you to come that you might bring us God. Oh, sir, do give us God." In that task also Christ shall not fail him! "Light shall shine out of darkness . . . the light of the knowledge of the glory of God in the face of Jesus Christ."[31]

CHAPTER SIX

THE CRAFTSMANSHIP OF THE PREACHER

CHAPTER SIX

THE CRAFTSMANSHIP OF THE PREACHER

THERE IS THE STORY OF A KING
who required of a famous artist an example of his
genius, and expected to receive some glowing canvas.
The artist, however, drew a perfect circle with one
sweep of his brush, and sent that as answer. A circle
seemed very simple—all too poor a demonstration of his
gift; yet to draw a perfect circle had levied the tax of a
lifetime's labor. A great sermon is likewise simple.
Hearing it, we say, "That is just what I have often felt."
Its ideas are transparent, its words are shining-clear.
Anybody could preach it. But, no! Preaching is both an
art and a craft. It may be learned, granted some initial
gift, but "not without dust and heat":

Let no man think that sudden in a minute
    All is accomplished and the work is done;—
Though with thine earliest dawn thou shouldst begin it
    Scarce were it ended in thy setting sun.[1]

This chapter will offer sundry comments on sermon-
izing. Their value, if any, will lie in the fact that they

are drawn from experience. They have fitness mainly
because they are first-hand. They are not new or novel.
But they may, perhaps, be written with a new accent;
and they must be written (if they are to have worth)
under the impact of a new age.

I

Is it necessary that texts and topics should be drawn
only from the Bible? We would answer that Jesus, our
prototype in preaching as in life, bowed to no such demand. The birds of the air and the sower going forth
to sow were His texts. Yet when He preached in the
Nazareth synagogue He expounded a passage from
the prophets. Furthermore, it must not be forgotten
that He is our gospel, and that He is portrayed in the
Book. Many have never found the Bible too narrow a
pasture. It is the world and everyman in miniature;
"the handbook of life," says Mr. H. G. Wells, "for
countless millions of men and women." The record of
the supreme religious insight of our race is there—there
in its progress and in its culmination. The fact that religious insight is there in its progress relieves us of
groundless dogmas of Scriptural infallibility, and gives
us new understanding of God's ways with men. The
fact that it is there in its culmination confirms us in our
faith that the Book has express purpose in the providence of God. Mark how the record of the Bible moves
from polygamy to a Christlike home; from prayer that

is a fear-stricken incantation to that Calvary-prayer of Jesus for His crucifiers; from child-slaughter to the "little child in the midst"; from a vindictive and local-ized deity to the "God and Father of our Lord Jesus Christ." Of the Old Testament we may well remember (lest we should count it a harp of broken strings) that Jesus sang its majestic psalms, and interpreted to His friends its deathless promises. As for the New Testa-ment it is more than a light to our path: it is life to our souls. Doctor Joseph Fort Newton has said recently that the rush of modern life with its jumpy and scrappy mind has made expository preaching well-nigh impos-sible.[2] If so, some of us are either accomplishing the im-possible or flying ruinously in the face of facts. But, as Doctor Newton doubtless intends, there is expository preaching and expository preaching. Beginning with the Bible, true expository preaching will carry it to life. But if we begin with life we shall end with the Bible, for the Bible is omnific. Doctor F. G. Peabody tells of some book in whose preface it is written: "The purpose of this book is that, being read, it may read you." The Bible reads us. No other book reads us half so search-ingly. A preacher need not be limited to the Bible for his texts. But if he stays within the Bible he will still not be limited, for the Bible has no limits. It might be added that topical preaching easily becomes repetitive and shallow. The preacher there exploits his own mood and interest, and is found threshing over and over the same old straw. We know of a minister who for several years preached against Christian Science and against the saloon *ad nauseum*. He drove several of his congregation to Christian Science; how many he drove to drink is not told. People have small concern for what the preacher does not believe, nor do they care much more for his partisan allegiances. Expository preaching, built upon a faithful study of the Book and applied with reality to life, will partake of the Bible's inexhaustible freshness and variety. It will be rich with the Bible's many-tinted glory; it will be fortified with the Bible's majesty and might. The Bible reads everyman.

2

But how are texts and subjects found? Students for the ministry are appalled at the thought of all the sermons they must preach. Years hence, if they are honest men, they will be still more appalled at the thought of all the sermons they have preached. Well do we recall how, a few days before the first Sunday in the first parish, we burned with a ruthless conscience the forty odd sermons written in our student days. The world is richer for that funeral pyre. Stillborn efforts most of them, not to be quickened into life by any measure of lusty smacking, and claiming only a decent cremation! Well do we recall how at the end of that first Sunday, the two new sermons having been preached, we were sure that there was nothing more to be said. The gospel

and the congregation were both exhausted. Since then
the truth of a wise old counsellor of those days has been
abundantly proved: "You will find that you are alongside a very deep well." But how are texts and subjects
found? They are not found: they come of themselves.
They jump from between the lines of the book you are
reading, though it may be a very secular book. They
look out at you through the mirror while you are shaving. They write themselves on the wall of the house
across the street. They tremble in the glow of evening
prayer. How come sermons?

> How to the singer comes the song?
> How to the summer fields
> Come flowers? How yields
> Darkness to happy dawn? How doth the night
> Bring stars? . . .[3]

Yet woe betide the man who presumes upon the gift
thus given in mystery! It does not come save by prior
consecration in labor and in life. The mystery is like
that of a harvest: it is not seen except in cultivated
ground. "The best preaching," says James Black, "is
always the natural overflow of a ripe mind"[4]—a mixed
metaphor, but no worse for that! If the well is not filled
all week by hidden springs of faithful study, the prim-
ing of the well on Saturday will be a creaky and exas-
perating process yielding only a trickle of living water
for thirsty lips when Sunday comes. Series of sermons

wisely planned will deliver the preacher from a frantic
searching for texts or from the vain endeavor to decide
between the rival appeals of several texts. They will
save also from unsuspected harping on one aspect of the
message. Such series should not have too many specific
topics—five or six is usually the wise number. The
Beatitudes, the Hilltops of the Life of Christ, the Char-
acters of the Passion Week, the Questions Jesus asked,
the Questions asked of Jesus, and many another series
will suggest itself.

Let the preacher's reading be constant. One hour so
spent each day will grant him the treasure of five or six
worthy books each month. He should read the Bible,
not merely for preaching purposes, but for the fructify-
ing of his own spirit. He should read it until he has
mastered it, until its music sings within him and its
pictures haunt his mind. He should read the great
novelists and the poets who stand high on the slopes of
the magic mountain. There are more sermons than the
Christmas Sermon in the works of Robert Louis
Stevenson. Robert Browning also stands in the suc-
cession of the prophets. The Russian novelists have a
poignant sense of the "still, sad music of humanity";
their answers to the great questions of sin and expia-
tion are never jaunty; for, as Doctor Hutton has said,
they realize that sometimes the arrow must heal in its
own blood. If science is the preacher's interest, he
should read science: it is the modern Aladdin's Lamp,

and some knowledge of science is necessary to every teacher in this age. If philosophy holds him in noble sway, he should read philosophy. A wise summer practice (if there is the good fortune of a long summer vacation) is the mastery of some one subject—the poetry of John Masefield, or the implications of biology for religion, or modern humanism. But, in any event, he should read big books, the books that must be read at the point of a pencil and that make the brain perspire. Reading for "homiletic bits" is the abomination of desolation. A brother minister told recently that there was only one good illustration in Amy Lowell's *John Keats!* There is no need to search for some fit punishment for such a man: he is his own castigation. Being "overtaken in one illustration, he flees unto another," and the breath of the pursuer is always hot upon him.

The preacher will profit by some system whereby this treasure of his reading can be preserved and made accessible. On that score we have no wisdom. Some ministers have elaborate filing methods. For us, such methods would be harder to remember than the information they are meant to hold. And it seems to us that when such ministers are preaching a discerning listener can always smell a card-catalogue in the offing. Doctor Kelman was wont to keep a "day-book"[5] in which he jotted down such passages or texts or ideas as he wished to keep. Gradually he found this material gathering around certain focal convictions which were the substance of his message. He listed these convictions, each under a word, and they became the index of his daybook. For ourself God has blessed us with a passable memory for what is contained in books (and for almost nothing else), and we read always with a pencil in hand, making our own index of each book on its back fly-leaf. To every man his own method.

3

How shall the sermon be prepared, when the would-be preacher has chosen his text—or rather when the text has chosen him? The text shall be studied in its setting, and a man must be honest with what he there finds. That initial study will ruin many a promising sermon; but it will give birth to more sermons than it slays. Is the topic "simplicity"? The topic is noble, even though the word is becoming "down at the heel." (Have you noticed how words rise in the world or fall on evil days? There is many a sermon in the history of words. Simplicity was once the "white flower of a blameless life"; now it is a half-wit doddering down the street.) "Simplicity" is the topic. The text obviously is: "The simplicity that is in Christ."[6] We search the context and find that Paul is warning the early Christians, not against a life of extravagance and display, but against being corrupted from "that single devotion that is towards Christ—unto Christ." Is that text

lost? No: it has given a new sermon; for Christianity is
just that "single devotion that is unto Christ." Perhaps
all true simplicity is none other than that same devotion.
With that initial study there must be a steeping of the
mind in the mood of the text; for every text in its context has its own particular mood or tempo.

The mood of the whole sermon will thus be determined—it shall have the rigor of a command, or a turbulent energy (as when Jesus ended a sermon, as nobody but Jesus would have dreamed of ending a sermon, in the words, "great was the fall of it"),[7] or the
tenderness of pleading, or the quiet intensity of some
ultimate insight into life. The mood of the sermon and
often its very form and outline are found within the
mood of the text. It is surely a prime necessity that the
mood of the sermon should be congruous with the
mood of the text. That is a canon of good preaching
not sufficiently stressed. The congregation is more susceptible than we think (perhaps more susceptible than
they think) to agreement or disagreement between the
bias of the sermon and that of the text. Let a man
beware of preaching in sedate charm on the text, "The
rains descended, and the floods came, and the winds
blew"![7] Nor can the forthright energy of life be well
discussed from the text: "Come unto me, all ye that
labor and are heavy laden";[8] if a man cannot feel tenderly compassionate unto very suffering, let him avoid
that scripture. If the text is a question, "And why even

of yourselves judge ye not what is right?"⁹ the sermon
may wisely ring changes on the question until it becomes inescapable. The cry of dereliction has its own
mood—sombre, awful, redly redemptive. Yet preachers have been known to use it as a convenient peg on
which to hang an argumentative discourse on the rival
theories of the Atonement, indicating meanwhile their
own likes and dislikes. That egregious insensibility
would find proper parallel only if a man should inter-
rupt the passing of the bread at Communion to discuss methods of farm relief. If the text pleads, the sermon should plead; if it sounds a challenge, the sermon
should sound a challenge. Through careful study a text
can be heard speaking, and almost dictating its own
message.

Then should follow a faithful study of that text in
the commentaries and in the more valid world of one's
own experience. The ideas that occur should be jotted
down, even if at first blush they seem to have scant
worth. There must be no waiting for the inspired moment: there is no inspiration for a lazy mind: God
helps those who help themselves. Happenings, quotations, paragraphs from this book or that will begin to
follow the text as the children in Hamelin Town followed the Pied Piper. Let the preacher fix them on
paper as they come. Within a day or two he will have
an amorphous mass of material, more than can be used.
Let that mass of material lie in his mind as now he

broods upon the text. Paul's wise advice (given before
any one spoke about "the subconscious mind") was
this: "Let not the sun go down upon your wrath."[10]
Go to bed in a bad temper, and that bitterness will
churn and curdle all the night; you will wake worse
than when you went to bed. The mind is not inactive
during sleep. Let the sun go down for a day or two
upon a sermon: the subconscious mind must play its
part. The man who procrastinates until Saturday does
not have that reinforcement. The man who sermonizes
betimes finds that life's mysterious powers are his
allies. The scattered bones of his preparation come together as in Ezekiel's vision—bone to his bone, and the
sinews come upon them and the flesh covers them.
The sermon takes form "he knows not how"—and the
form is proper and indigenous.

But in all this study let the imagination have large
liberty. The imagination that is licensed yet unthwarted
is a preacher's indispensable ally. Many a promising
sermon is stultified because it is woven of concepts
rather than of pictures. John Ruskin's words are here
most pertinent:

The greatest thing a human soul ever does in this world
is to *see* something, and tell what he *saw* in a plain way.
Hundreds of people can talk for one who can think, but
thousands can think for one who can see. To see clearly is
poetry, prophecy, and religion—all in one.[11]

A sermon beginning in some simple incident at once enlists the attention. We find that the sermons of the great preachers almost always betoken a visual imagination. Not quickly shall we forget how Doctor John A. Hutton convinced a congregation that lawlessness in private conduct ends in public disaster. He imagined every automobile driver following his own whim concerning one-way streets, the passing of traffic-lights, the right side of the road, and a desirable speed. Before the illustration was complete he made an erstwhile advocate of personal liberty climb to the top of a hill of wreckage and address the world in general on the merits of social control. The preacher must think in pictures! Even an adjective, if it is the inevitable adjective, is usually a picture—as when Tennyson writes of "the *leprous* sycamore." He must cultivate the imagination. He must project the Bible incidents onto the screen of his mind. The greatest thing a preacher "ever does in this world is to see something and tell what he saw in a plain way."

4

Then must come the writing of the sermon. But must a man write? For ourself (we would not dogmatize for any other man) that question is answered in emphatic assent. The sermon must be written—not as an essay is written, but as a sermon is written; that is to say, with the eyes of a congregation (wistful, hungry, sad, or gayly indifferent) looking at the writer over his desk. Such writing is not an easy task. There will be days when the pen will not move. Preaching is a great art, akin to the painter's art. Every artist knows times when the spirit is inert and the travail of the mind seems barren. These dead hours, with futile struggle for their only life, can be a pain worse than physical pain. They are the cross by which alone, even in preaching, a man may attain unto the resurrection from the dead. The sermon, at least according to our own conviction, must be written.

Only so can a proper balance be achieved. The introduction can then be made brief as it must be—its phrases terse and vibrant; not pitched in too high a key lest the continuance of the sermon should seem an anti-climax, but warm with human interest, linking the text to present life. The proportions of the sermon in its different pleas or emphases can be preserved. The "transitions" (and how important they are!) can be made smoothly. A congregation has some right to know where a preacher is travelling. He should at least indicate the mile-stones. But some preachers, instead of indicating the mile-stones, dig a trench across the road (which is a fair description of a long and awkward pause or a clumsy transition), and the poor congregation must scramble out of the trench before it can resume the journey. It is often wise to allow a congregation to sit down awhile on a mile-stone and rest. A judiciously placed and chosen illustration will serve that purpose. In a written sermon, furthermore, the prosy paragraphs can be detected and excised. The message can be carried in a steady ascent, with now and again a "rest" in the gathering urgency, until it reaches its culmination. The appeal at the end can be made searchingly, tenderly, with finality—a pleading for a verdict in the court of the soul.

Only in a written sermon can the illustrations be properly placed and aptly phrased. A trite illustration may creep in unchallenged in the heat of extempore utterance; it will creep out shamefacedly from a manuscript that is under scrutiny. With a world "so full of a number of things," with the kingdoms of literature and science beckoning the explorer, with life (decked in rich colors, its pulses beating high) knocking at all the doors, a trite or hackneyed illustration is almost beyond pardon. A colleague told recently how at an American Legion Convention a veteran of the Great War appeared on the platform and asked this one question: "Can anybody tell me who I am?" He was suffering from lapse of memory. The preacher would be sterile in fancy who could not lay such an incident under fee. In a recent novel, the hero is in the grip of a carnal imagination, and this phrase is used of fleshliness: "It is like a recurring decimal."[12] Three into ten goes three times, and there is one "over." A naught is added. Three into ten goes three times, and there is

still one left over. There is everlastingly one left over!
There is no deliverance!—"like a recurring decimal."
With so many thrilling illustrations beckoning to the
preacher if his eyes are open (if he is living for people
through his task) bathetic illustrations are ruled out
of court. How many fine instances are within every
man's reach! A sermon without illustrations is like a
house without windows. A sermon with trivial or
bathetic illustrations is worse: it is like a house with
the windows broken, and the holes stuffed with rags
and straw.

Only in a written sermon can the thought be clarified, and the diction cut until it shines with facets like
a jewel. Again we would be emphatic: the preacher's
thought must be clarified. Over and over again he must
demand of himself: "What do I wish to say?" Ideas
that are vague to himself will be confusion worse con-
founded to his hearers. "Deeds not words," we have
said, is a muddled proverb. Words are deeds—the deeds
of the lips. The warning spoken by Jesus should be for
ministers like the handwriting on the wall: "And I say
unto you, that every idle word that men shall speak,
they shall give account thereof in the day of judgment.
For by thy words thou shalt be justified, and by thy
words thou shalt be condemned."[13] How many idle
words there are in the average sermon—words that do
no work, that are not felt, that are merely sound! Let
the sermon be written, and when it is written, let the

redundancies be pruned away with an unsparing hand. Let the commonplace phrases be given short shift. Let them yield place to phrases that glow, that move in the imagination like a drama. Let the cumbersome words of Latin origin be pushed aside: they make any style lumber along like a procession of elephants. There are Anglo-Saxon words of one syllable (staccato words like "sin," haunting words like "home," ultimate words like "God") that grapple the heart with hooks of steel. Let the long sequences of juicy adjectives be cut away. A florid phrase is florid. A bare phrase may have beauty —like the tracery of winter trees. One adjective is better than six, and none is often better than one. If one is used, it must be so germane as to appear wedded to its noun. Of twenty adjectives that will serve, one conveys the subtle shade of meaning. That one will not be found except by the discipline of the pen. Roget's *Thesaurus* and Webster's *Dictionary* should be always at a minister's elbow. They are poor masters but invaluable friends. This question of diction and clarity is not academic: it is moral! A preacher is under indictment who does not ask and answer these questions: "What do I wish to say? Why do I wish to say it? How can it be said with vividness, compulsion, and tenderness?" Doctor Coffin has told that for years it was his practice to write at the head of his manuscript the aim of that sermon: "I wish and am required in this sermon to . . ." Such clarity of aim will blaze a straight trail through many a listening mind. Read the parables of Jesus: mark their simplicity, their charm, their abrupt challenge, their stab of surprise. Even through the opaqueness of a translation and the prison of a printed page, Jesus is revealed as a Master-interpreter. Or consider the diction of this poem, with never a cloudy word, or a freakish word, or a cumber-some word:

> I do not think that fields and meadows are
> Moral, or that the fixity of a star
> Comes of a quiet spirit, or that trees
> Have wisdom in their windless silences.
> But these are all invested in my mood
> With trust and strength and fortitude;
> That in my troubled season I may cry
> Upon the wide composure of the sky;
> And envy fields, and wish that I might be
> As little daunted as a star or tree.[14]

It is unhappily true of Romanist worship that it is phrased in an alien tongue. The congregation hears only strange sounds—as though Christ were exotic or remote. Vigilance is required lest that charge should be made of Protestant worship and preaching. Though couched in our English speech, they have not always been guiltless of the charge. The first translator of the Bible into English resolved that his version should be plain to the man behind the plough. The preacher must be a good shepherd of words. That good shepherding will help him to be a good shepherd of souls.

Let the sermon be written. If it is not written on paper, it must be written just as scrupulously on the tablet of the mind.

5

Assuming the sermon is written, how shall it be delivered? Shall it be read? Few preachers and fewer hearers would answer, "Yes." There have been great preachers who have read their sermons. "Chalmers," says Doctor Cadman, "wrote like a giant and read as Jehu drove";[15] but genius is subject to no convention. A read sermon is doubtless preferable to extemporaneous speech if the latter is slipshod and ill-prepared; but in most churches a manuscript even dramatically read would be a barrier between preacher and people. Then shall the manuscript be memorized? Doctor A. J. Gossip takes issue with those who would reply in too dogmatic a negative. He reminds us that Disraeli and John Bright in their early days both learned their speeches by rote, and tells a delightful story of the guests at a country home fleeing from one corner of the garden where Hugh Cecil was declaiming a forthcoming oration only to find themselves beset in the next shady nook by Winston Churchill practising his peroration.[16] But such memorizing is beset by pitfalls. A few individuals might walk through the hazards unscathed, but most men would succumb. They would fall on this side into the pit of stiltedness or on that side into the deeper pit of unreality. The mind cannot safely be divided between a congregation and a photostatic copy of a sermon printed on the page of memory. In this question of delivery each man must discover his own method. For us, writing is inescapably part of it. After that, the manuscript can be mastered (not by rote but in substance) and left at home; or it can be taken into the pulpit as a guide-map; or it can be condensed into notes brief or full and the notes used as a prompter. In any event the preparation must be painstaking, and the sermon must be mastered.

As to voice and manner preaching needs no *ex cathedra* attitude. It is killed by pontifical tones. It is doubly killed by a martyred voice, as though the preacher were the sole defender of the faith and sore bestead. Many an otherwise good sermon is spoiled because the preacher is constantly "pressing" (to use golf parlance). If he is unrelievedly insistent, hammering away at the congregation, they will emerge not healed, but spiritually black and blue. Scolding is equally anathema: one flashing phrase that cuts like a rapier is better than an orgy of denunciation. Purple patches of eloquence should be under suspicion; purple patches in any event do not shine gloriously unless they are set in the familiar background of the common earth. The belaboring of a topic and an audience is probably the most prevalent fault. It sometimes comes of the preacher's unavoidable tiredness, and may be

pardoned; but more often it comes of incomplete preparation. The man who arrives at this task unprepared
deserves to suffer the penalties, but it is a tragedy that
the congregation should suffer in his guilt, and that the
word of life should be dulled or torn.

6

Now let it be said that all these means and methods
might almost be cast to the winds so long as preaching
is real; and that if preaching is not real every method
becomes a broken reed or an offence. If a sermon does
not carry an unmistakable accent of reality, then, even
though every rule is honored, that sermon will be
vanity and vexation. Why do men use a pulpit voice?
It is not *real*. No voice is real except a man's own voice.
When the voice of an ordinary man can, with training,
be made orchestral in its treasures of modulation and
color and appeal, why should a man intone?—or why,
being an ordinary man, should he thunder and declaim
as though he were an archangel trumpeting the oracles
of heaven? A pulpit voice is not *real*. Why do preachers
play the sedulous ape, imitating other preachers, when
every man has his own gift? That imitation is not *real*.
Why do they use phrases drawn from old theologies
which were vital to our fathers (because born of their
experience), but which oftentimes are not vital to us?
It would be well for every preacher to be compelled to
answer such questions as these: "What do you mean by

'grace'?—by 'coming to Jesus'?—by 'being saved through His blood'?" Unless these phrases mean something in actual experience, and mean something tremendous, it were better that he should not use them, for such phrases are then not real. One of the best of many good stories told about Doctor A. J. Stalker[17] is of his prayer on a Sunday morning when the weather was enough to try a saint. His congregation knew his sincerity, and knew how constant and genuine was his gratitude for temporal mercies as well as for spiritual gifts. But how could he offer any thanks for daily cheer on such a day? There were inches of slushy snow underfoot and a persistent drizzle everywhere else. Would he do the formal thing in his prayer? Would he, for once, say what he did not feel? He began to pray in an utterly honest voice: "O Lord, we thank Thee that it is not always as bad as this"; and with that he continued as honestly, until his people were lifted above their rainy gloom into a rapture of gratitude. But of so many sermon-phrases it must be said: they are not real. And why (the questions are growing harder, and the thrust of them deeper) do preachers, who remain immured in their studies, discuss problems and sufferings with which they have not come to grips, and in which they have not lived? That discussion is not *real*. And why do preachers so glibly say more than they know about God, and about loyalty to Him, and about prayer? It is so easy to say more than we know! It is so appallingly easy to burn with a false passion for righteousness as though it were true! Better far that the preacher should confess his sins to his people than pretend even by inference to a consecration that he does not know. That glib speaking about God is not *real*. Defects in preaching skill and sins in preaching method will all be pardoned, if the man himself is sincere and if his very voice rings true.

The preaching of the New Testament has conquering reality. There is no escaping its sincerity and conviction. Great preaching in every age has shared and reiterated its invincible actuality:

That which was from the beginning, that which we have heard, that *which we have seen with our eyes,* that which we beheld, and *our hands handled,* concerning the Word of life (and the life was manifested, and we have seen, and bear witness, and declare unto you the life, the eternal life, which was with the Father, and was manifested unto us): that *which we have seen and heard* declare we unto you also, that ye also may have fellowship with us: yea, and our fellowship is with the Father, and with his Son Jesus Christ: and these things we write, that our joy may be made full.[18]

CHAPTER SEVEN

THE PERSONALITY OF THE PREACHER

CHAPTER SEVEN

THE PERSONALITY OF THE PREACHER

THERE ARE SIX OR SEVEN
theological students each year doing "field work" in our
church. "Field work" is an ironic term to use of New
York's east side: the work is there but not the fields.
These students, could you know them, would give you
abounding hope for the ministry in the next generation. It may be found, when the books are balanced,
that the best gift of that church to the kingdom has
been (despite many more noticeable gifts) its share in
the training of students. This little group holds a seminar with one or other of the ministers of the church
each Sunday. He tries to teach them; they assuredly
teach him. When his work has been shaken in the sieve
of their valid criticism, there is not much of it left.
Shaking is good for the liver; and many of a preacher's
troubles lurk there—in the liver of his self-regard.

I

At one seminar we discussed the secret of a minister's
influence. These men used the word "influence" in its

best sense. They are quick to recognize cheapness, and
they despise it. They are not misled by numbers or popu-
larity. What is the secret of real influence in a preacher?
—we asked. Is it physical vitality? That is a factor, we
agreed; it gives red blood to a sermon, and infects the
listener with health and cheer. Is it mental keenness?
That also is an asset: a sharp intellectual scythe is better
in the time of harvest than a dull blade. But these questions left us still on the circumference of the quest. Two
men of equal energy and equal mind might be imagined
preaching the same sermon: in the one case it might
fall dead at his feet, and in the other flame like a torch.
Character, then—is that the answer? Not in any ob-
vious meaning of the word: two preachers might be
of equally good character, so far as eye could judge, and
one carry conviction and the other leave his congregation almost inert. We searched for the subtle factor
of difference, and found only that the search is vain.
It goes to the *deepest roots* of character. Nay, it goes
beyond the man to the pleasure of God. But they were
sure (these fine men foresworn to the preacher's calling) that the purity of a man's motives outweighs all
other elements in his influence and almost cancels out
other factors of difference.

To that conclusion these chapters have compelled us
—though until now it has not been written. Words are
a most potent weapon, we have said; perhaps they are
earth's most potent weapon, because they of all weapons

are most freighted with personality. But suppose the personality is shoddy? We have found also that authority is, in final analysis, Life—the quality of life that is in Jesus. But suppose the preacher lacks that quality of life? We have suggested, further, that the notes of authentic preaching in our day are earnestness, compassion, cheer, challenge, unequivocal reality, and the mediation of the sense of God. But these are not features of a typewriter, a pen or a page: these are the marks of a man. John Milton has words about a poet that are even more true of a preacher:

He who would not be frustrate in his hope to write well in laudable things, ought himself to be a true poem . . . not presuming to sing high praises of heroic men or famous cities, until he have in himself the experience and the practice of all that is praiseworthy.[1]

The seminar of which I write left us with that sobering truth—namely, that a man with every other gift may yet be "frustrate in his hope" to preach, if his secret life is not itself a sermon. We prayed that night as men rarely pray. We prayed feeling, with Abraham Lincoln, that there are times when there is nothing else to do. We found that Pentecost is more than a story in a Book.

2

"Be yourself" is current slang; but, rightly understood, it is good counsel for the preacher. God chooses to speak through men. "The heavens above and the

earth beneath" also praise Him, but in fullest sense of
speaking these do not speak. Francis Thompson, going
to nature's treasures for his comfort, makes that confession: "Their silence is their sound."[2] God speaks His
best truth in and through human life. "The Word became flesh, and dwelt among us."[3] Not only so: God
chooses to speak through "ordinary" men—and may
He forgive the adjective! He takes some Gideon from
the field—the least man of the most obscure family of
the least celebrated tribe of Israel. When He would
kindle His fire on earth, He turns a bramble-bush into
lambent flame: the bush burns and is not consumed,
and the whole mountain-side is holy ground:

> So with the Lord: He takes and He refuses,
> Finds Him ambassadors whom men deny,
> Wise ones nor mighty for His saints He chooses,
> No, such as John, or Gideon, or I.[4]

There is, in strict fact, nothing commonplace in the
God's world. The replicas, the drab samenesses, have
come from man's hand by mass-production. God does
not manufacture: He creates. "One star differeth from
another star in glory."[5] Every leaf of a tree is variant
and distinct. Likewise every man is another man. He
has his own finger-print, his own ectoplasm (if you
will!), his own accent of voice and soul. One possession
we do not hold in common—our personality. That is
our best capital. That also is the medium of the preacher's best service.

Let it be said without careful searching for phrases: the world is tired of the cleric: it demands to hear the man! "He is a typical minister," the world says; and therein is our condemnation. We are decorously and conventionally the same. We are echoes and imitations. We are servile to our own fashion in an age that (while boasting its freedom) is appallingly servile to its fashions. We are "typical ministers"! Our one separate possession we barter away for conformity to type. "Do you know who I am?" said the nobleman, swelling with importance, to the boy who failed to tip his cap in the lane: "I am the marquis." "An' does yer honor know who I am?" said the lad. "I'm Patrick Murphy from the cabin by the bog."[6] The world will not listen (and why should it?) to a man who will not speak with his own voice and look through his own eyes. The preacher must indeed be meek; but meekness, as Charles Rann Kennedy has told us, has its own terrible strength. In surrender to God it has gathered His power—not to the blotting out of its distinctive traits but to their enhancement. Of personality also the paradox of Christ is true: he that is willing to lose it for His sake finds it accentuated and redeemed.

Ultimately our only gift is the gift of ourselves. In all our preaching we shall not say anything new; and how many can hope to say it as well as Horace Bushnell and Phillips Brooks have already said it? Yet, we may say it with our own turn of speech and our own

turn of mind; and, if we are genuinely living in our
times, we may say it to a new age. One criticism lev-
elled at Jesus is that He said nothing new, that His every
saying can be found in near-parallel in the Judaistic
faith in which He was reared, or in one or other of the
ethnic faiths. Nor can that contention easily be gainsaid. Yet the contention is of comparatively small moment, for He gathered the sayings into a new mosaic;
He built them into a new temple. That final word,
"Thou shalt love thy neighbor as thyself"[7], He lifted
from the ruck and rubble of the Levitical code, and
made it a cornerstone. There was a new proportion and
emphasis in His teaching. Moreover, He baptized every
saying in His own spirit, and from those waters of
baptism every saying rose with a morning radiance.
"Thou shalt love thy neighbor as thyself"—but *His*
love was unto a Cross (and that love was new), and
His neighbor was everyman (and that neighborliness
was new). Originality, as we may one day learn, does
not live in the letter—"the letter killeth." It lives in the
mood, the association, the emphasis, the spirit—and
"the spirit maketh alive."[8] The preacher of to-day cannot speak a new word, for there is only one gospel.
But, by virtue of the new self God has given him, he
may speak with a new emphasis and a new mood. He
may be like Peter, dashing and impetuous—and fool-
hardy; or he may be like John, clear-eyed, intense,
with great deeps of soul; or he may be like Thomas,

analytical, rational, finding faith at the last in a love he cannot withhold. Jesus never chose a man for his discipleship who was content to be a pale copy. "It seemed good to me also,"[9] said Luke—and that is his account of the origin of a gospel. He had not been an eyewitness. He had not been an Apostle. He was, perchance, not even a Jew. Yet he was resolved to bear his individual witness. He must needs tell of One who reigned in his life with a most winsome love—and what loss to our world if he had failed in false modesty to speak his word!

In our boyhood, stories were current of a certain Joseph Spoor who would stand with one leg on the pulpit chair and the other on the reading-desk, and with a roll of papers would illustrate his conception of the trumpet-call on the Day of Judgment. We do not commend that kind of originality (it is easy to mistake bluster for brains, and cheapness for distinctiveness), but even that kind of genuine selfhood would be preferable to intoning like a machine as though preaching were a treadmill dreariness. A wise preacher will study the masters, but he will not mimic them; he will be himself. Not that he will keep his people on tenterhooks fearing what he may next say and do. We have heard of one minister concerning whom our informant told us that she dared not close her eyes at any dinner at which he asked the blessing: she wished to be open-eyed and fortified against whatever shock or whimsy he might that day perpetrate. A man may do the conventional thing without stultifying himself! The truly original people do not shatter in their every utterance the accepted forms of speech and outlook; they pour into the old forms a new life—the wine of the personality God has given. Nothing is much more distressing than to see a minister aping another minister—an aping which invariably ends in an emasculation—as though God had made him a parrot instead of a man. "There came a man, sent from God, whose name was John."[10] There came a man, sent from God, whose name was ———. You may set your own name there. There is only one you. There is a word that only you can speak. There has been no other "you" since time began; there will be none till time ends. Pray that the word of your life may be fully spoken.

3

But granted every man's instrument is his own, the music is Christ's—and it has always its dominant notes. We speak now of the octave not of preaching but of personality.

In his private character (if any character is private!) the preacher will be *courageous,* with a many-sided courage. He will courageously set his face against cheapness in his ministry, and against the delusion of short cuts to the success of his commission. He will have courage to be simple—with the simplicity that can walk with kings "yet keep the common touch," and which, keeping the common touch, still is kingly; the simplicity that in its message sounds depths for the learned, yet is plain to the lowly in mind. He will have courage to resist the lure of ecclesiastical ambition, and to judge his ministry by a higher test than church statistics. He will have courage not to dangle a bait to catch a crowd (that method may fill a church, but usually it retards a kingdom), and courage not to confine himself to the elect. He will not leap from the pinnacle of the temple to dazzle all eyes; neither will he pose there to show that the rarefied climate of the skies is his native air. He will have courage neither to worship the crowd, nor to fear them, nor to despise them: but to love them. He will have courage to fill an obscure place faithfully—ashamed that he should ever ask wider opportunity than One who, treading a little conquered country, made it a Holy Land; and who asking of mankind no more than a Cross on which to die, transfigured it into the talisman of our salvation. Such high courage must mark the ambassador of Christ!

The preacher as a man will be *sympathetic*. We require of a novelist that he shall understand life. We ask of a doctor that he shall know our frame, saying, with diagnostic finger, "Thou ailest here—and here." Likewise the world would declare of its preachers: "Come, see a man, who told me all things that ever I did;[11] everything that ever I needed, and desired, and must become!" Sympathy is no shallow grace easily acquired. To "side in" with people, to say what they in their self-pitying wish us to say, is easy. But to speak the truth without harshness is not easy. A recent book[12] describes a woman ill, but not seriously ill; and surrounded with many tokens of a happy life—by the devotion of her family, the gifts of her friends, and the amenities which money can buy. Yet she is whining over her pains, and wishing in effect that "the Lord Jesus would take her." Harshness would say: "Good thing if the prayer were answered!" Sentimentality would perjure itself and say: "You are a terrible sufferer, and wonderfully patient." Sympathy would say—what would sympathy say? Truth, assuredly!—though with that winsomeness not found except in Christ. But sympathy goes far beyond the speaking of true words—or, rather, the words will not be true unless they come from a travail of spirit. What to say to one who after his wife's death finds that she has over the years been faithless? What to say to one who has just heard from the doctor that his days are numbered? What to say to one who has made a havoc of his human chance? What to say? Nothing—until the preacher as a man has, by dint of resolute imagination, first lived himself into that person's need and there discovered for himself a resource. Nothing to say—until the preacher knows that, if he were in that actual encounter, he could lift a banner above it and prevail. Have you ever offered a sympathy which, in the very sound of it, betrayed the defencelessness you would feel if you were in that sorrow? Genuine sympathy is more than a "feeling with" (though that grace is high, and hard to win): it is a "conquering over" in a Presence newly sought and newly found. Sympathy is not an easy gift.

The preacher as a man will be *sincere* (*sine cera* in the Latin: "without wax" in the stone) so that when the sun's rays shine on him there will be no long-hidden deformities suddenly come to light. Is the preacher the victim of his moods? All men of sensitive soul have that besetment. Even Hugh Latimer, who bravely died a martyr, confessed:

> For I am sometimes so fearful that I would creep into a mousehole. Sometimes God doth visit me with His comfort. So He cometh and goeth.

Every fine-grained spirit has that shine and shadow, but he will not be victimized thereby if he is wholeheartedly Christ's. While he has light he will walk in the light; and while he has darkness he will walk in memory and conviction of the light until the light returns. We do not discuss at length those other cavities filled with the wax-of-pretense which God's sun would reveal. The querulousness of moods is one of them; making sermons about the good life a substitute for living it is another (a substitution easy to commit and equally easy to hide from ourselves); the carnal imagination, evil cousin to religious fervor, is another; the winning of a spurious success, hating ourselves for it but refusing to disavow it, is another. Enough! We need not undress our souls. "I have become aware of a stinginess in myself," said Boswell to Doctor Johnson. "So have I," retorted the old doctor; "but I shall not blab about it." If we are aware of the wax-filled gaps we need not blab about them. There are matters best left undissected except in the place of prayer—and not to be morbidly dissected even there. Enough to realize that a minister cannot carry conviction an inch beyond what he knows and lives. People look at us on the street and say: "Has he found it—this joy and power of which he preaches?" Their real quarrel with us is not the quarrel exploited in the magazines: the real quarrel of the world with the preacher is that we ourselves do not appear vital with the life we so confidently proclaim. That criticism does not figure in the magazines—to print it would be confession of the world's own haunting sense of need. "Has *he* found Life?"—such is the world's real question about us. The preacher must be sincere.

The preacher as a man must have *faith and passion*. With what abounding hope Jesus went about the world: "According to your faith be it done unto you";[13] "Only believe; all things are possible to him that believeth."[14] He was sure of God's transforming grace. He expected to see renewals and deliverances beyond sight.

There was a Universe of power accessible to men through Him, if He kept the faith—a Niagara of light and power there at the contact-point of His lips and hands and eyes! So He believed. So, in marvellous truth, it was! He spoke with faith and passion.

Does the preacher of to-day live in that same faith and passion? Does he expect (yea, and claim of God) that when he is preaching he may then and there open the door of some man's dungeon so that he shall say with Masefield's "Saul Kane":

> O glory of the lighted mind!
> How dead I'd been, how dumb, how blind![15]

Does he expect that through him God may sweep away another man's selfishness in a sudden wave of love, so that he shall say:

> I knew that Christ had given me birth
> To brother all the souls on earth![15]

There is hardly a finer picture of a preacher's passion than that of George Whitefield on the evening of his death. Preaching two hours in the morning (with no other visible girding than his passion, for he was almost too weak to stand), the crowd assembled that evening before the door of the house where he was staying, and thronged the hallway impatient to hear the man they loved. "I am tired," said Whitefield, "and must go to bed." He took a candle and was going to his bedroom, when the sight of the people moved him. He paused on the staircase and began to preach. The crowd looked up—and he preached. There was something (nay Someone) whom he must give; some veritable power and mercy for them through him; he *must* speak. He preached until the candle went out in its socket. That night he burned out the candle also of his own life— which shineth always.[16] Have we that faith? Have we that passion?

4

We forbear the further telling of those "marks of Christ" that we as preachers and as men should bear branded on us. We know Him well enough to know His marks. But "who is sufficient for these things?"[17]

We ourselves, from the vantage-point of our own wisdom and will, can move toward that sufficiency.

The physical care of ourselves must not be despised. Jesus lived out of doors, and slept on the ground; and we do not read of His being ill. The disciples also were hardy men who knew the tang of wind and wave. There is not one flabby or mushy line in the gospels. Bodily health affects preaching. Calvinism under John Knox would have been a happier theology had he not been somewhat neurotic. If you keep old sermon manuscripts (a practice which to one man may be of God) the mere reading of them after lapse of years is enough to teli you whether your brain and body were physically vigorous when you wrote this or that or the other sermon. Here are Ian Maclaren's rules of health for the minister:

> . . . to have his study recharged with oxygen every hour, to sleep with his bedroom window open, to walk four miles a day, to play an outdoor game once a week, to have a six weeks' holiday each year . . . all that his thought may be oxygenated, and the fresh air of Christianity fill the souls of his people.[18]

Again, a minister may learn (even if he is not studious by native bent) to be scrupulously faithful in his preparation. There are ways and means by which a parish becomes informed that its minister expects, for the sake of the church, that morning hours shall not be invaded by small personal demands or trifling parish emergencies. The church we know best frequently prints in its Sunday bulletin a notice to that effect; but a capable secretary as outpost and a long-suffering but tactful wife as Horatius at the bridge are the best defence. Granted, however, that the morning hours are free, there must still be the will to use them. The newspaper is a snare, and desultory reading is a pitfall. How many of us really *think* in genuine sweat of mind? Reading can become a substitute for thinking. There is the story of Shelley's time-schedule: "I study Portuguese while shaving. I translate Spanish for an hour before breakfast. I read all the forenoon and write all the afternoon; every minute of the day is filled with something"; and an old Quaker woman answering him, "Friend, when does thee do thy thinking?" To study what we ought to study—digging into the treasure of the Bible, brooding over a sermon until it "comes alive," contemplating Jesus until year after year He becomes more radiant and inescapable, keeping abreast of the epochal books that reveal to us the mind and mood of the time, and the rigorous discipline of the pen whereby this labor and listening are transcribed into our best words—is a man's task! But how such a task, faithfully done, would kindle mind and heart! Of such travail are born faith and passion, courage and sympathy!

The ditch-digger works eight hours a day, and thus helps to liberate the minister to *his* toil. The preacher can ride—if he is unworthy enough—in a rickshaw carried on the backs of sweating men. The doctor often works twelve hours a day. Some business men make a great show of working, and others *do* work. Some of the most energetic work at the making of money with a zeal that puts to shame the children of light. A minister is master of his own time. Who knows whether he is working when he is behind study doors? He may be indulging in a comfortable reverie. Does he really work eight hours a day—or twelve? It is a besetting sin with ministers to talk about how busy they are and how overworked.

And those afternoon hours—are they honorably employed? If we went into four homes a day for five days each week and for only forty-five weeks of the year we would make at least the beginnings of friendship in several hundred homes. And if, in each home, we "lived where they live"—not by any gaucherie or unwarranted probing, but by a genuine friendliness that wins its own trust and confidence—what blessing might be there! The many "meetings" we could afford to let languish; the committees could by themselves labor like a mountain and bring forth a mouse; the organization could have fewer wheels within wheels, spinning busily but so often ungeared to worthy tasks: it would not matter! Meetings and organizations are so often that Gehazi-staff: life is quickened only by direct impact of personality on personality.

Faithlessness in the week's work will show like a blight when Sunday comes—for it is a blight. But faithfulness is its own strong faith. It breeds its own convictions. "Light is sown for the righteous."[19] We never cross the ocean and watch a sailor at work without wishing that our work in the "Great Taskmaster's eye" could be done with as much thoroughness, as much out-of-sight effectiveness, as much prompt yet quiet meeting of emergencies, as much fine indifference to danger, and as high a code of honor.

5

In short, we are required to live a disciplined life. We cannot keep every pleasure, or the mind will become chaotic. We cannot read every book—what athlete would dream of eating every food? And if we would be free of sin we must forego the habit or the interest in which that sin is embedded.[20] So often we ministers speak as if we could be rid of some unworthiness without any surgery. Not so have we learned Christ. The insidiousness of sin is that it becomes entangled with— nay, ingrained in—an avocation or a pursuit otherwise commendable. There is then no getting rid of the sin by any tweezers or pin-point method. Perhaps the avocation or the pursuit itself must go, however commendable —in a surgery so ruthless that Jesus called it cutting off a hand or plucking out an eye. All this (need it be said?) not for any gruesome purpose of self-thwarting but rather that the river of life, blocked here and there and there, may carve its own straight channel and move impetuously and with strong depth to the sea.

There was once a Man who lived the life. He was peasant-born, and met nobody of "importance" save John the Baptist. The historians, had they mentioned him, would probably have dubbed him "a religionist from Galilee." He was killed by people inwardly blind. But He lived the life. We have written of the Fourth Gospel as "interpretation," a portrait in oils (rather than a photograph) displayed to the mind of the world at the end of the first Christian century. But what had He to do with Grecian philosophies and Gnostic heresies at the end of the first century? Oh, He lived the life! His Cross is now against the skyline of almost every modern city. But what has He (that Craftsman from the hills of Galilee) to do with our cities? Oh, He lived the life! "There are also many other things which Jesus did, the which, if they should be written every one, I suppose that even the world itself would not contain the books that should be written."[21] "Strong hyperbole," says the learned commentator—which shows that a learned commentator may be as blind as a bat. "Many other things which Jesus did"—yes, He is always doing things. He has never stopped doing things. He was working in the life of the author of the Fourth Gospel, working in St. Francis, working to-day in Albert Schweitzer; working in the broadening of our creeds, our protest against civic shame, our sword of the Spirit lifted against the sword of war; and working in you and me just as often as we dare to think of Him. How could books begin to tell what He has done? All because He lived the life! This vast issue from one consecrated soul!

Suppose we should dare to live the life? Already we have met more people than Jesus met. We have points of contact and means of influence denied to Him. Suppose we came clean before God; suppose we were really ready to be killed for an inner Something more dear than life; suppose we took our chance with Him! The secret of preaching is in the surrender of the preacher to Christ.

6

But the question returns: "Who is sufficient for these things?" Our faithfulness and self-discipline may carry us some distance toward that sufficiency; yet, when we have done all, what a continent remains between us and the mark of our high calling! But if we cannot move far toward the goal, the goal may move toward us! God is not a vast inertia: ". . . his father saw him . . . and ran"[22]—do you remember? The Father embraced his son before the son had a chance to speak in confession.

> Think you, 'mid this mighty sum
> Of things for ever speaking,
> That nothing of itself will come,
> But we must still be seeking?[23]

The goal of sufficiency "of itself will come"—if we pray! "If we pray": therein is the forgotten secret of Christ. Our record of Him is so fragmentary that not more than one hundred days (perhaps not more than sixty days) have any mention. Yet we read repeatedly that He went into a mountain to pray. Three times we' are told that He spent half the night in prayer. He prayed at His Baptism, at the tidings of the death of John the Baptist, at the coming of those Greeks who seemed to Him the first fruits of a world-wide harvest, at the Last Supper, in the Garden of Gethsemane—and on the Cross. At every crisis of joy or sorrow, at every onset of new responsibility, at every crucial decision, at the sounding of every new challenge—He prayed. He prayed for others—for little children who were brought to Him "that He should lay his hands on them, and pray";[24] for Peter—"but I made supplication for thee, that thy faith fail not";[25] for His disciples—"I pray not that Thou shouldest take them from the world, but that Thou shouldest keep them from evil";[26] for all mankind—"Neither for these only do I pray, but for them also that believe on me through their word";[27] for His enemies—"Father, forgive them; for they know not what they do."[28]

Is this the preacher's forgotten secret? Have we, with all our efficiency, omitted the one effectiveness? And why does the "social gospel" forget that it was born and reared in prayer, and cannot without prayer hope to survive? Helmholtz, the scientist, when asked how he came by some brilliant hypothesis, answered, simply: "It was given to me." George Eliot avowed of certain intense and vibrant passages in her novels that they were dictated to her rather than written by her. Life is an inlet, filled, for those who wait and pray, by ocean-tides of power.

Coleridge's nephew writes thus of the poet:

My uncle, when I was sitting by his bedside, very solemnly declared to me his conviction on this subject. "Prayer," he said, "is the very highest energy of which the

human heart is capable": prayer, that is, with the total con-
centration of all the faculties. . . . "To pray," he said, "to
pray as God would have us pray,—it is this that makes me
to turn cold in my soul. Believe me, to pray with all your
heart, and strength, that is the last, the greatest achievement
of the Christian's warfare on this earth. Lord, teach us to
pray!" And with that he burst into a flood of tears and besought me to pray for him! Oh, what a light was there![29]

It is of that incident that Alexander Whyte makes his
comment.

Prayer is far too princely a life for most men. It is high,
and they are low, and they cannot attain to it. True prayer
is colossal work. There were giants in those days. Would
you be one of this royal race? Would you stand in the lot
of God's princeliest elect at the end of your days? And
would you be numbered with His Son and with His choic-
est saints? Then, PRAY.[30]

Browning has that same truth dramatically given in
a poem called *Instans Tyrannus*. He tells of a tyrant,
and of a small man who troubled him just because he
was so small. It is both art and truth that Browning
should choose the smallest man and link him with
prayer to show prayer's power. That smallest man irked
the tyrant as a mosquito might have irked him:

> I struck him, he grovelled of course—
> For, what was his force?
> I pinned him to earth with my weight
> And persistence of hate—
> And he lay, would not moan, would not curse,
> As his lot might be worse.[31]

What to do with that man? He would have given him riches and taken them away, but the man was not to be tempted by riches. He would have seized his kith and kin, and thus played the tyrant; but the man had no kith and kin.

> No! I could not but smile through my chafe—
> For the fellow lay safe
> As his mates do, the midge and the nit,
> —Through minuteness, to wit.[31]

Yet he was resolved to wreak senseless vengeance on him (the man vexed him so), even at cost of half his realm:

> So I soberly laid my last plan
> To extinguish the man.
> Round his creep-hole,—with never a break
> Ran my fires for his sake;
> Over-head, did my thunders combine
> With my under-ground mine:
> Till I looked from my labour content
> To enjoy the event.
>
> When sudden . . . how think ye, the end?
> Did I say "without friend"?
> Say rather, from marge to blue marge
> The whole sky grew his targe
> With the sun's self for visible boss,
> While an Arm ran across
> Which the earth heaved beneath like a breast
> Where the wretch was safe prest!
> Do you see? Just my vengeance complete,
> The man sprang to his feet,

Stood erect, caught at God's skirts, and prayed!
—So, *I* was afraid![31]

Jesus had not where to lay His head. No wealth could
tempt Him. Every friend forsook Him. Rome trod on
Him at last as a man treads on a moth. Trod on Him?
Just when the earth's unprovoked vengeance was complete, He caught at God's skirts and prayed! He lived
the Life. Nay, He *prayed* the life, and redeemed His
race from sin to God!

To pray in a faith which says, "God is. Only He is
great. He wills to live and work through me. If I renounce every secret ambition alien from Christ, I may
become the living contact-point of His life"—that indeed is colossal work, but through such prayer colossal
forces of hope and healing are released. Then all life
moves with us. There is the story of an Arctic expedition in which men had plodded on in utter weariness to
make no apparent headway. But when they took their
bearings they found themselves nearer their goal than
they had dared to dream: the ice-country on which they
plodded had itself been moving, carrying them on! Our
wisdom and will are poor enough; but the very ground
of life is in God—and that ground of life moves as we
move, if we pray in His name.

"How shall we escape, if we neglect so great a salvation?"[32] How can we fail if we are thus consecrated to
His calling and girded by His power?

Chapter Eight

THE PREACHING OF THE CROSS

CHAPTER EIGHT

THE PREACHING OF THE CROSS

APOSTOLIC PREACHING HAD but one word—Christ. Apostolic preaching linked to that Word one overmastering adjective: "Christ *crucified.*"

Did they not preach a risen Lord? Yes; but the way to the open tomb, they said, was the way of the Cross; and the power that burst the bonds of the tomb was Calvary's seeming weakness. Apostolic preaching pictured Jesus in Heaven breaking the clasps of the book of life's mystery. No one could open that book. It was held inscrutable in the hand of "Him that sitteth on the throne." But Jesus opened it and made known its glad tidings that death is a dark angel and pain an ultimate love. Jesus was able to open it. Why? Because His hands were *pierced* hands! Now the song of the redeemed swells and breaks and swells again like a resounding sea: "Worthy art *Thou* to take the Book . . . for Thou wast *slain.*"[1] Always in apostolic preaching there is that one accent on the one word Christ: "For I determined not to know anything among you, save

Jesus Christ, and him crucified."[2] "But far be it from me to glory, save in the Cross of our Lord Jesus Christ."[3]

Modern preaching, judging it in its whole range, has lost that accent. If you are brave enough to read the sermon-topics page in the Saturday newspaper (and you will need to be brave: it is a modern chamber of horrors), you will not find there much promise of sermons about the Cross. Even among the honest titles (we mean those not trying to inveigle people into church on false pretenses) Calvary finds scant place. Why is it? Our easy view of sin is a contributing cause. Our forced optimism also, in which we resemble the king who banished sackcloth from his palace thinking he could thereby banish sorrow. Our externalism makes us strangers to the Cross in its unplumbed depths. Our self-sufficiency of material wealth and mechanical power blinds us to our dependence on God and to that spiritual poverty in which we must trust only in His mercy. A modern writer quotes with apparent assent:

> I fight alone, and win or sink,
>   I need no one to make me free;
> I want no Jesus Christ to think
>   That He could ever die for me,[4]

as if mothers did not die for us, and teachers, and soldiers, and doctors, and the God within! It is almost incredible that any one could be so blind to the vast "givenness" under which we live.

Nor has the Church been guiltless in this neglect of the Cross. Harsh theories by which the death of Christ is a price paid by God to the devil have alienated the moral sense of mankind. Bewildering theories which require a jugglery within God's nature, the Cross being a "satisfaction" which God in His love makes to Himself in His holiness, have left men dazed. Arbitrary theories, whereby a guiltless Christ is on Calvary reckoned guilty of our sin, have left men repelled; for no one can be made guilty of sins he has not committed, and God last of all would wish to make him guilty. A man may bear the penalty of sin, and wear the shame, and make common cause with sinful men; but, being guiltless, he cannot be made guilty; otherwise the universe would be in its morality a topsy-turvydom. Theology, dripping with "the blood" almost to soul-revulsion, has made the Cross unreal. It is not blood that saves, but blood as life outpoured; and only the holy compassion of the life outpoured can give redemptive virtue to the blood. The Cross stands in the midst of life. In the words of a fine title, it is *The Crucifixion in Our Street;*[5] nor is it short of tragic that the Church should have lifted the Cross out of life and set it in the midst of a strife of theological tongues to make it a fiction.

There is a commendable reason withholding reverent men from the preaching of the Cross: we are utterly unequal to it both in mind and soul. Can we cup an ocean in our hands? Nay, can we tread even with sermon-shoes where the place is holiest ground? Doctor Henry Sloane Coffin has recently reminded us that John Milton wrote of Christ's nativity (and how gloriously!), but that when he tried to write of Christ's Passion he abandoned the attempt with this note:

> This Subject the Author finding to be above the years he had when he wrote it, and nothing satisfied with what was begun, left it unfinished.[6]

The preacher hardly dares to begin this preaching and must always "leave it unfinished." Yet he must begin. In a Cathedral at Lucca there is a crucifix said to have been carved by Nicodemus—so clumsily carved that he left it in despair. But (says the story) in that despair an angel came while he slept and made the crucifix true both to the eye of the craftsman and the eye of the worshipper. A Spirit can thus redeem our poor preaching of the Cross. To such preaching we must pledge ourselves. Let the history of the Church be for a witness that power has visited the Church in such preaching, and that power has ebbed when the Cross has been forgotten. In any event love compels us to cry —it is all such preaching need hope or wish to say— "Behold the Man!"

I

The magnetism of the Cross so strangely persists as to indicate a miracle. For why should any one to-day trouble himself about a Peasant hung in an obscure land many centuries gone? Why should any one dream of making His death a sermon? What the Jews thought about a man thus slain you may know from their ancient law:

And if a man have committed a sin worthy of death . . . and thou hang him on a tree; his body shall not remain all night upon the tree, but thou shalt surely bury him the same day; for he that is hanged is accursed of God; that thou defile not thy land. . . .[7]

"Take him down!" the law said; "or he will turn the very ground sour!"

Rome would not crucify a Roman, not even the meanest of her citizens. She kept that death for the alien and the enslaved. It was the final venom of His foes, that Jesus should thus die. A very few might have been so foolish as to love Him in life, but who could love Him in death? They had quenched His light in dark shame! Had they? When His sun set, the night did not conquer it. His sun in its setting tore asunder the blackness and brought a new, strange day. Suddenly this gallows, by His dying upon it, ceased to be the implement of shameful death and became the symbol of—Life! And this is a miracle. If by miracle is meant a shattering of all probabilities, an apparent disrupting of uniform sequences, the Cross of Christ is a miracle.

We preachers in our preaching may forget the Cross;

but the world cannot forget it. The novelist Thackeray was walking one day to the west of Edinburgh when he suddenly saw the wooden crane of a quarry standing as if etched against the sky. He stopped, gazed intently, and then said in an awed voice: "Calvary!" Could the Jews of Jesus' day have conceived of such an incident, or the Greeks have imagined that after many generations an illustrious man of letters would bow in reverence before the gallows on which a Carpenter died?

What a strange persistence lives in the Cross! Mr. M. L. Fisher tells in a sonnet how once he caught a glimpse in a Museum of Art of a sculptured head of the Crucified. He could not forget it. He must find it again. In his search he passed by cloths of gold, jewelled robes that kings had worn, famous pictures, carven gems. He had no eyes for these, eager only for one Face. Wherein is the power of Calvary? He admits that power and states it, though he has no explanation:

> The World is old; she hath seen many wars;
>   And states and kingdoms crowd her courts like grass;
> Princes in pride she watches where they pass
>   Unnumbered and innumerable as the stars;
> Then turns, a child with tired feet homeward set,
>   Back to the Cross, and lo! her lids are wet.[8]

Why preach the Cross? Because the world has felt with a true instinct that life is there! Forsaking the Cross, the world has always come back to the heart's home. Despite our contentious theories, mankind looks to Calvary as to some secret of power and hope.

2

Why the preaching of the Cross? It would be more than enough to answer: "Because Jesus Himself pointed to the Cross and chose it as the red heart and culminating act of His mission on earth." As we trace His psychological journey we can see how He tried honorably to avoid it. His inner struggle, as well as Peter's blindness, is revealed in the words, "Get thee behind me, Satan."[9] We can see how, as often as He tried to escape the Cross, he returned to it. He asked, even at the very end, to be spared it; but, finding it unavoidable in any honor of the soul, He chose it. Beware of any theory that would argue that He did not choose it. He could have avoided it; He chose not to avoid it. "I have power to lay down" my life,[10] He said grandly. "If any man would come after me, let him deny himself, and *take up* his cross. . . ."[11] Jesus took up His Cross: nobody forced it on Him. He chose it because, by some premonition of His soul, He saw in it our world's salvation. Ever and again in what Franz Liszt called the "madness and the exultation of the Cross" He would exclaim: "I, if I be lifted up from the earth, will draw all men unto me."[12] That was His faith. Strange faith! Those were saner words, or so our world would judge, spoken by a father to his son:

Have patience for awhile, my lad,
Dream no more i' the quiet night
Forever since the world went mad
Lads have dreamed to set it right.

. . . .

Of old a dreamer strove to mend
The mad world's warp with his white hands,
And lo, as every dream doth end,
So ended His with lash and brands.
The mad world sat and drank and diced,
And, as a dreamer hath no friend,
He hung alone above the lands
And dreaming, died; his name was Christ.[13]

Did the dream end? Others have dreamed of world
dominion: conquerors of subduing mankind by a
sword; statesmen and ecclesiastics of binding mankind
in an iron system; poets of winning mankind by a song.
But here was a Carpenter dreaming of dominion by
His death! He asked only a Cross on which to die in
love! "Nail me to your gallows, if it must be," He
cried; "and the world will be God's!" If to Jesus the
Cross was the winning of the world to God, dare we
leave it unproclaimed?

Explain it as we may, the magnetism of the Cross
endures and grows. By some quirk of history, or some
providence, or some inward law, the death-gallows of
that Galilean Peasant in a remote and inconsequential
corner of the earth, has cast a healing shadow over
every land. The world may not like it. The world may

say it darkens life with stern demands, may deride it as the symbol of a morbid sentiment, or protest against it as a jarring discord in our rightful joys; the world may cast all trammels to the winds, vow the vow of freedom, and denounce the Cross as a foolish and cruel self-mutilation: its maddening power remains!—a gallows dismissed by Pilate with a gesture and hated by the Jews as a badge of deepest shame, now come to strange life, now etched against the skyline of every city, now carried at the forefront of every human march as though, somehow, the issues of life and death are in it. In our moments of vision we turn from the tantalizing mirage of pleasures and greeds like

> . . . a child with tired feet homeward set,
> Back to the Cross, and lo! (our) lids are wet.[8]

It almost seems as though the crazy dream were coming true!—"I, if I be lifted up from the earth, will draw all men unto Me."

3

How can we explain the magnetic force of Calvary? "It is merely the natural outgoing of sympathy in face of suffering," comes the reply. But is it merely that? Sympathy soon ebbs: it does not endure for two thousand years. If sympathy is the explanation, why do we not reverence three crosses instead of one? The thieves also were crucified. Thousands have died heroically, agonizingly, and have been forgotten. Thousands more notable in earthly rank than Jesus, far more conspicuous on the earthly stage than He, have died in martyrdom; but their death is not taken as a universal symbol. Socrates was condemned to death unjustly, and as he drank the hemlock cup he defied his foes to catch his soul. Then why erect a Cross above the grave of our dead? Why not place there instead a carven replica of a hemlock-cup?

"Dogma has sustained the Cross," somebody suggests. No, the Cross has sustained dogma—some of it such poor dogma that but for the tenderness of the Cross it would long ago have perished. "The early disciples got it into their heads that Jesus was alive after death," another voice proposes; "and then they began to weave weird doctrines of propitiation by His blood." That account is plausible: its only defect is that it raises a hundred questions for every one it answers. Why should the disciples "get it into their heads that Jesus was alive," when they were mourning Him as dead? And why should they find in a hanged man (who would turn the ground sour if they did not take Him down) the propitiation for their sins? And why do poets write about Him still? Why does one of the most recent of them, known to some as coldly intellectual, thus ask:

> Friendless and faint, with martyred steps and slow,
> Faint for the flesh, but for the spirit free,

Stung by the mob that came to see the show
The Master toiled along to Calvary;
We gibed him, as he went, with houndish glee,
Till his dimmed eyes for us did overflow;
We cursed his vengeless hands thrice wretchedly,—
And this was nineteen hundred years ago.[14]

"*We* gibed Him?" "*We* cursed His vengeless hands?" Verily! For, whether we like it or not, the Cross has become cosmic, *because Christ is cosmic*. The Cross is ever-present, because Christ is ever-present. He shall see of His travail. According to His faith it shall be done unto Him. He, being lifted up, shall draw the world to Himself and God. We have no other gospel but Christ and Him crucified.

4

Then what shall be our preaching of the Cross? It shall not be as a theology, save as theology is life. It were wise in this preaching to eschew theological terms, that we may tell in simple speech of a "crucifixion in our street."

Preach the Cross as the revelation of God, as the one clue in an often unintelligible world. A fine phrase in the Old Testament reads thus: "Yet the soul of my lord shall be bound in the bundle of life with Jehovah thy God."[15] But life is a disconcerting bundle. There is woodland in it "flecked with leafy light and shade," and in the woodland reptiles and poison berries. There is children's laughter, and children slain by contagious disease. It is a world of sunrise and earthquakes, of poems and wars, of saints and devils, of birth and death. Life is like a palimpsest—writing over other writing, scribbled and garbled, erased and written again beyond all deciphering. Where is the clue? Nothing there but a farrago of bright and dark, straight and twisted, making—nonsense!

But one sentence is clear—the record of the days of Jesus!—

> With this ambiguous earth
> His dealings have been told us. These abide:
> The signal to a maid, the human birth,
> The lesson, and the young man crucified.[16]

In all the entangled writing, one record is clear. Stamped deep into the whole palimpsest is the sign of a Cross! God is in the life of Jesus. Of that we are sure—by whatever theological formula we may choose to describe Him. If His life is not instinct with God we would almost prefer not to know God: we would rather trust Christ. But if Jesus revealed God by His living, He revealed God also by His dying—for His life and His death are woven in one piece. If the life of Jesus is a window through which we see God, the death of Jesus is such a window giving us a deeper vision.

In an Italian church may be seen a picture of unwonted insight. At first glance it is only another picture of the crucifixion. But a second glance shows it to be different: there can be seen a vast and shadowy Figure behind the figure of Jesus. The nail that pierces the hand of Jesus goes through to the hand of God. The spear that was thrust into His side is thrust also into God's side. Thus does the crucifixion become a clue. "If God were good," says the world, "the sin of the earth would break His heart!" to which the preacher answers, pointing to Calvary, "See His breaking heart!" "If this kind of a universe with its griefs and graves is somehow necessary for our growth, then God, if He were good, would at least share its pains with us," says the world; to which the preacher answers, pointing to that strange Man on the Cross: "See God sharing our pains!" "If God is God," the world says, "then in compassion He will bear our sins as only God can"; to which the preacher makes answer: "Behold Him bearing our sins! Behold in Calvary a focus in time and space of that travail which God bears from the foundation of the world". . . . There in the Cross is the clue which, followed, leads us to the assurance that the heart of life, however mysterious, is yet kind.

5

Preach the Cross as the way to life—as the best wisdom of human conduct. Ultimately the only wisdom is one that will teach us how to live. Most questions find no answer in theory: they receive their "yes" or "no" only as we live obedient to some high surmise. The Greeks laughed to scorn the self-mutilation of Jesus, and the Jews recoiled from it:

> Go, bitter Christ, grim Christ! haul if Thou wilt
> Thy bloody cross to Thine own bleak Calvary!
> When did I bid Thee suffer for my guilt
> To bind intolerable claims on me?
> I loathe Thy sacrifice; I am sick of Thee.[17]

So they might have spoken in that day. So we might speak. But it remains true that character is made by its choices, and that life compels us to the choice.

However the choice may be described, the many selves within us are grouped in form of an alternative —a higher and a lower. We may seek near, visible gain; or we may seek far, invisible gain. We may grasp; or we may give. We may stay on the safe side of the Pillars of Hercules, or we may sail the untracked ocean. And life compels us to the choice—on that we may be dogmatic. Jesus was writing a footnote to history as well as uttering His own verity when He told us that it is not possible to play life both ways: "Ye cannot serve God and mammon."[18]

Usually we call the lower nature "myself," as in the couplet:

> And ah for a Man to arise in me
> That the man *I* am might cease to be![19]

Similarly Samuel Rutherford identified himself with his lower nature.

> Oh, that I were free of that idol which they call "Myself," and that Christ were for "Myself." . . . But that proud thing "Myself" will not play except it ride up side by side with Christ, or rather have place before Him. . . . Nay, when I am seeking Christ and am out of myself, I have a third part of a squint eye upon that vain, vain thing "Myself." . . . Oh, would to the Lord I had not a "Myself" but Christ; not a "my ease" but Christ; not a "my honor" but Christ.[20]

Thus we can call our poorer self "myself." Jesus taught us otherwise. He said of the prodigal that he was not himself when he went to the far country. "When he came to himself" he turned homeward. Sometimes we catch this fine optimism of Jesus, and say of our friends when they are "fratchy" (that's a provincial English word, but you can hear what it means!): "He is not himself to-day." It is a strong first stroke in this inward battle to tell ourselves that we, the real "we," are always our higher selves. But—here is the inescapable fact: If we cleave to the lower self, we lose both that and the higher; for we keep company with the ghost of a slain nature that is more truly us —and keeping company with that spectre we are forever distraught. But if we cleave to the higher self, we must cut away the lower even though by a painful surgery. Would we excel in learning? We must "scorn

delights and live laborious days." We cannot live in
the higher without crucifying the lower. All worthiness has its thorn-crown, its spear-point, its nails, and
its cry of dereliction. By its cross it comes to its kingdom. What seemed to be self-mutilation proves self-
enhancement. "He that loseth his life . . . shall find
it."[21]

In the Boston Library there is the famous picture
showing young Galahad approaching that high throne-
seat which was said to rob a man of his life. The motto
was carved on that chair: "He who sits herein shall lose
himself." As Galahad moves forward we can see the
knights of the Table Round make the sign of the Cross
with their uplifted sword-hilts. An angel draws aside
the red coverlet from the chair. We can hear Galahad
saying: "If I lose myself I save myself." Christ by His
Cross has sealed for us that best wisdom of conduct.

6

Preach the Cross as God's power. How is the Cross of
Jesus the power of God? We would not need to ask
if our ideas of power were not honey-combed with
falsity. Power to us is brute force. Usually it does not
occur to us that there can be other kinds of power.
"Power for what?"—that question is pivotal. A famous
journalist in his column remarked that Mr. Frank B.
Kellogg had now signed his eightieth peace treaty.
This, he allowed, was a matter of rejoicing; but a few

score new battleships and a few hundred new battle-planes would be cause for much greater rejoicing. His assumption was that peace-treaties and the mood which prompts them have no power, but that battleships and battle-planes have immense power. But power for what?

We are anxious that our children shall grow up joyous, clean-limbed, eager-minded, true-spirited. All we need is power. Then call in the electric hammer and the steam-shovel; in them is power to spare. Ah, but no power to make a boy or girl grow as Jesus grew. Or we would be free from the intolerable load of our sins. All we need is power. Then call upon one of those new battleships. It has power. Yes, but—power for what? Power to blast, but no power to forgive! No power there to make an enslaved will walk in freedom! No power there to lift the cloud of sorrow! No power there to make a friendly earth! When all the blasting has been done, somebody must begin to build. Only love can build. . . .

The Cross—God's power! But power for what? If God's purpose is to make men and women kind and true, then removing mountains into the sea and plucking stars from the sky (such wonders as the world has always required of its Messiahs) are a waste of time. New battleships are worse than a waste of time. What will make people Christlike? The Cross, for instance! There is always the Cross! Love laying down its life—

parents for their children, patriots for their country, laborers doing it for us at what seems to be the price of their nobler growth, poets scorning surface gains and living deep, philanthropists pouring forth their gifts, doctors and prophets and teachers. On all these there is the mark of the Cross—love laying down its life. To make people Christlike there is no other power—only the power of loving life laid down. If that is God's purpose then the truest sign of God's strength will be the *sign of God's own life laid down!* The only ultimate power will be God's life laid down! "Therefore we preach Christ crucified—the power of God."

7

Preach the Cross as salvation from sin and unto life eternal. We shall not waste time to argue that we need forgiveness. If we do not sense that need, no argument will help us. Indeed, we are most of us too conscious of our own sins to dream that we have much right to talk to other people about theirs. Shallow minds may say that sin is nothing—a trifle, an immaturity, a besetment we cannot avoid. But the saints have not so described it: their pages are blotted with tears and twisted with anguish. Nor have the great dramatists or the great novelists so described it. Macbeth in Shakespeare's drama, with blood of murder on his conscience, asks a doctor to

Raze out the written troubles of the brain.

There is an illness no drugs or surgeon's knife can cure. Jesus did not describe sin as a little thing: "If thine eye causeth thee to stumble, pluck it out. If thy hand causeth thee to stumble, cut it off."[22] Thus Jesus spoke of sin. It was the one enemy to be feared: "Be not afraid of them that kill the body"[23]—death was not to be feared; but sin was to be feared as its own hell.

Doctor Henry van Dyke has argued that there are two ways among others by which we may know that sin is real—by the judgment of regret and the judgment of condemnation.[24] Is there anything we regret? Do we ever say: "I wish I had not done that!" or "I would give anything to blot out the record of that day"? Such regret is an acknowledgment that we could have done differently, that sin is real. And is there anybody we condemn? Or do we say of brutal men: "They could not help themselves. It has been intended from the foundation of the world that grafters should fleece the innocent"? We know what is wrong! The judgment of condemnation is the sufficient sign that sin is real.

It is so real that it cannot be imprisoned in the life that commits sin: it spreads through the human family. One man stained the name of Judas—and now no mother would think of calling her child by that name: any child called Judas is under suspicion. One minister or doctor drags his name in the dust—and the finger of suspicion is pointed at every doctor or minister.

One man breaks into a house—and everybody must put locks on the doors, pay taxes for protection, and sleep uneasily. How sin spreads! Men have always thought of it as like a stone dropped into water: its ripples move in ever wider circles—perhaps through every land, perhaps through every succeeding age. Do we ever see the end of a sinful act or thought?

Then how shall sin be overcome? How shall it be forgiven? By the red law and strange sacrifice of suffering. If we read history simply to stuff the mind with facts we may miss that law; but if we brood over history we cannot miss it. How are the frontiers of man's habitation advanced? By pioneers lost upon the ocean, lost behind the ranges, lost in arctic snows! How is our health won? By men like Doctor Robert Koch who found that sleeping sickness was caused by the tsetze fly, and that the fly drew its venom perhaps from the blood of crocodiles; and who therefore penetrated the jungle and lived on an island in the midst of an infested lake to study the disease (yea, and to expose himself to it) at its source. How are the liberties of mankind purchased? By men like William Lloyd Garrison, honored now as "The Liberator," but who was so poor at the first that he slept on his printer's table, and who twice was mobbed—once by the best society of Boston. How are the harshnesses and the money-madnesses of our industrial order overcome? Children once worked from five in the morning until seven at night in English cotton mills until men like Shaftesbury pleaded their cause. "What means are taken to keep you at your work so long?" these children were asked. "There are three overlookers," they replied; "there is one head overlooker, there is one man kept to grease the machines, and there is one kept on purpose to strap." Meanwhile the best thing his enemies could say of Shaftesbury was that he was "the advocate of a misplaced and perverted humanitarianism." If you wish that matter brought down to date (it is so easy to choose illustrations at a convenient distance in history!), we shall say that the iniquities of *our* industrial system will be banished—our money madness, our exploitation of humanity by monotony of toil, our indifference to recurrent unemployment which is a part of the system—only as there are those willing to bare their backs to the lash of obloquy and to be called "radical," "sentimentalist," and "fool"; only as there are those willing to be stricken not only from the "black list" of certain embattled organizations but from the society of folk apparently gentle and discerning.

We cannot tell why the redemption of mankind should always be at such cost. Sometimes we find it in our own heart to doubt the goodness of a God who can make His world fair only through tragedy. We have said with Francis Thompson:

> Ah! must—
> Designer Infinite—
> Ah, must Thou char the wood ere Thou canst limn with
> it?

.   .   .   .

Whether man's heart or life it be which yields
Thee harvest, must Thy harvest fields
Be dunged with rotten death?[25]

We cannot tell why the world must climb by such painful steps. Why anything is, and why anything is as it is, are the ultimate mysteries. We cling to the faith that if there had been any other way for God to bring us to a perfect stature, any better way than the way of sacrifice, He would have chosen it.

But the red law is there! The teacher shedding blood of mind for the scholar; the mother daily dying for her child; the doctor and nurse bearing pain that others may be free from pain; the just yielding up life for the unjust—there is no mistaking the law. Our choice is really very simple: we may laugh our way through life keeping our eyes steadfastly away from its pain, or (on the same side of the alternative) we may become one of the intelligentsia and condemn the world as a God-less riot of injustice—or we may say as Jesus said: "Ought not a man to suffer? If sharing a load can lighten it, ought not a man to get under the load?" Just two alternatives!—to stand on the sidewalk and with smiles or despair watch the procession of man's agony go past black with crosses, or to volunteer to carry one of those dark burdens.

We can fulfil that law for one another, and we must. But that fulfilment is not enough. For—though the mother may atone in suffering for her children, the teacher for his scholars, the doctor for his stricken brethren, the patriot for his country, the philanthropist and social servant for his needy comrades—there still will be need for some one to pay the price for the mother, the teacher, doctor, patriot, philanthropist, since these are themselves not without sin. And that suffering Spirit must be vast as humanity—for the consequences of sin run out through all lands and all generations. Who shall meet the bitter cost for all mankind?

Who but God Himself? He only is good enough, kind enough, vast enough in power, enduring enough in time. His suffering must save mankind from age to age. He must be the "Lamb slain from the foundation of the world."

Is there sign of such a God, a *living* sign, a *functional* sign? Yes, on Calvary! There is the red heart of the Christian gospel! A Man was found good enough to need no remission for Himself, compassionate enough to gather a world in love into the arms of a Cross. That Man is now the Saviour of mankind.

> I know not how that Bethlehem's Babe
>   Could in the God-head be;
> I only know the Manger Child
>   Has brought God's life to me.
>
> I know not how that Calvary's Cross
>   A world from sin could free;
> I only know its matchless love
>   Has brought God's life to me.[26]

There, on that hilltop, the heavens opened to reveal God. There we learn that the Man who obeyed the dark mystery of suffering is the only Man who ever was really at home in life. There we can hear the redeemed in a "far, spiritual city" whose gates are like a Cross, singing of their Leader returning from His wars:

> But, lo, there breaks a yet more glorious day:
> The saints triumphant rise in bright array:
> The King of glory passes on His way.[27]

How can we preach at all if we preach not the Cross? At long last, what else is there to preach in this kind of a world? We must say, again and again, "Ye were bought with a price."[28] We must say until the words haunt the mind and become their own peace:

> O dearly, dearly has He loved,
>   And we must love Him too,
> And trust in His redeeming blood,
>   And try His works to do.[29]

"We preach Christ crucified." God forbid that *we* should glory save in the Cross of Christ our Lord.

NOTES

NOTES

CHAPTER I

1. I Corinthians 1:21.
2. Charles Silvester Horne, *The Romance of Preaching.*
3. Alfred Tennyson, *In Memoriam,* canto cxxiv.
4. Donald Hankey, *A Student in Arms,* page 190. (Dutton.)
5. John 1:13.
6. Robert Browning, *Dramatis Personæ, Epilogue.*
7. Alfred Tennyson, *The Poet.*
8. Isaiah 6:5.
9. I Corinthians 9:16.
10. James 3:6. See James Moffatt, *The New Testament, A New Translation.* (R. R. Smith.)
11. Matthew 12:37.
12. Luke 21:33.
13. Gamaliel Bradford, *Damaged Souls,* pages 13, 14. Used by permission of Houghton Mifflin Company.
14. I Thessalonians 4:18.
15. Matthew 12:36.
16. See A. J. Gossip, *In Christ's Stead,* pages 33, 34. (Doran.)
17. Mark 1:14.
18. Robert Browning, *Rabbi ben Ezra.*
19. Matthew 18:20.
20. Mark 13:32.
21. II Timothy 2:15.
22. Matthew 13:54, Mark 6:2.
23. Robert Browning, *Love among the Ruins.*
24. Matthew 11:29.
25. John 10:7.

CHAPTER II

1. Colossians 4:1.
2. Philippians 2:7.
3. Romans 2:16.
4. Hebrews 12:3.
5. Frederic W. H. Myers, *Saint Paul,* included in *Collected Poems.* Used by permission of The Macmillan Company, publishers.
6. F. T. Palgrave, a hymn beginning, *Thou say'st 'Take up thy cross.'*
7. William Shakespeare, *Measure for Measure.*
8. Rudyard Kipling, *The Explorer,* included in *The Five Nations,* copyrighted 1903 by Rudyard Kipling. Used by permission of the author and Doubleday, Doran and Company.
9. Robert Bridges, *The Testament of Beauty.* Used by permission of the Oxford University Press.
10. Matthew 7:24.
11. Matthew 5:10, 11.
12. Matthew 11:28.
13. Matthew 5:21, 27, 33, 38, 43.
14. J. Middleton Murry, *Jesus, Man of Genius,* page 8. (Harpers.)
15. *Ibid.,* page 23.
16. Matthew 3:13–17.
17. I Peter 2:22.
18. John 8:46.
19. Mark 3:14.
20. J. G. Whittier, *Our Master.*
21. John 16:12.
22. John 1:14, freely translated.
23. Eunice Tietjens, *The Great Man.* Reprinted by per-

mission of and special arrangement with Alfred A. Knopf, Inc., authorized publishers.

24. John Drinkwater, *To and Fro about the City*. Used by permission of Houghton Mifflin Company.

25. Kahlil Gibran, *Jesus the Son of Man*. (Knopf.)

26. Bruce Barton, *The Man Nobody Knows*. (Bobbs, Merrill.)

27. William Ellery Leonard, *The Poet of Galilee*. (Viking Press.)

28. Upton Sinclair, *They Call Me Carpenter*. (Regan.)

29. Evelyn Underhill, *The Mystic Way*. (Dutton.)

30. J. A. Robertson, *The Spiritual Pilgrimage of Jesus*. (Doran.)

31. Friedrich Rittelmeyer, *Behold the Man*. (Macmillan.)

32. Walter Russell Bowie, *The Master*. (Scribners.)

33. Robert Browning, *Dramatis Personæ, Epilogue*.

34. These criticisms of the ethic of Jesus are well summarized and answered by Dean Inge in *Christian Ethics and Modern Problems*, chap. 2. (Putnams.)

35. Acts 4:12.

36. This contention is convincingly stated in *The Place of Jesus Christ in Modern Christianity*, chap. 9, by John Baillie. (Scribners.)

37. Louis Golding, *Second Seeing*, included in *The World's Great Religious Poetry*, page 325, edited by Caroline M. Hill. (Macmillan.)

38. J. Middleton Murry, *Jesus, Man of Genius*, page xii. (Harpers.)

39. Luke 12:57.

40. J. Middleton Murry, *Jesus, Man of Genius*, pages 371, 372. (Harpers.)

41. Frederic W. H. Myers, *Saint Paul*, included in *Collected Poems*. Used by permission of The Macmillan Company, publishers.

CHAPTER III

PREACHING CHRIST TO THE MIND OF TO-DAY

1. Robert Browning, *A Grammarian's Funeral*.
2. Matthew 10:34.
3. I think this phrase is Walter Russell Bowie's, although a search has not discovered it in his writings.
4. Matthew 13:52.
5. Sophocles, The *Antigone*.
6. Matthew 6:27, Luke 12:25.
7. Psalm 97:11.
8. Matthew 5:5.
9. Psalm 119:97.
10. John 8:36.
11. Matthew 5:21, 27, 33, 38, 43.
12. Matthew 16:3, Luke 12:56, freely rendered.
13. Robert Louis Stevenson, *If this were Faith,* included in *Complete Poems.* (Scribners.)
14. Matthew 7:26.
15. John Masefield, *The Everlasting Mercy,* included in *The Everlasting Mercy, and The Widow in The Bye Street.* Used by permission of The Macmillan Company, publishers.
16. Let confession be made: the reference for this incident has been mislaid, and to discover it again might involve the re-reading of the novels of the author in question. Presumably the quotation is from *The Sky Pilot* by Ralph Connor. (Revell.)
17. Alfred Noyes, *Watchers of the Sky.* Copyright, 1922, by Frederick A. Stokes Company. Reprinted by permission.
18. John 5:44.
19. Alfred Tennyson, *In Memoriam*.
20. Robert Browning, *Bishop Bloughram's Apology*.

21. Mark 9:24.
22. Quoted from *Thoughts on Religion at the Front,* by Neville Talbot. The quotation occurs in *The Roots of Religion in the Human Soul,* page 28, by John Baillie. (Doran.)
23. Francis Thompson, *The Hound of Heaven.*
24. John 16:33.

CHAPTER IV

PREACHING CHRIST TO THE SOCIAL ORDER

1. A. B. Belden, *The Greater Christ,* page 128. (Judson Press.)
2. *Whither Mankind?* page 97, edited by Charles A. Beard. (Longmans.)
3. At a meeting of Sigma Chi in New York City before whom a rough draft of this chapter was read, and to whom I am indebted for many criticisms and suggestions.
4. Joseph Fort Newton, *Things I Know in Religion,* page 124. (Harpers.)
5. Luke 4:25-27.
6. Mark 12:40, Luke 20:47.
7. Matthew 21:13.
8. Matthew 23:27.
9. Matthew 10:17.
10. John 17:19.
11. E. L. Bogart, *Direct and Indirect Costs of the Great World War.* (Oxford.)
12. Matthew 26:45 and parallel passages.
13. See also the author's *The Parables of Jesus,* page 134. (R. R. Smith.)
14. W. M. Clow, *The Cross in Christian Experience,* chap. 19. (R. R. Smith.)

CHAPTER V

PREACHING CHRIST TO THE INDIVIDUAL OF TO-DAY

1. A. B. Belden, *The Greater Christ,* page 128. (Judson Press.)
2. Judges 6:34.
3. Isaiah 32:2.
4. Elizabeth Barrett Browning, *Aurora Leigh.*
5. Mark 3:14.
6. John 7:48.
7. Job 16:4, personal possessive pronouns reversed.
8. Louise Driscoll, *God's Pity.* Used by permission of The Macmillan Company, publishers.
9. John 4:35, freely rendered.
10. Matthew 4:19.
11. II Kings 4:31.
12. W. Fearon Halliday, *Psychology and Religious Experience* (R. R. Smith), who quotes from Alfred Moll's *Hypnotism.*
13. Walter Lippmann, *A Preface to Morals,* page 113. (Macmillan.)
14. Alfred Tennyson, *The Making of Man.*
15. Halford E. Luccock, *Jesus and the American Mind,* page 102. (Abingdon Press.)
16. Alfred Tennyson, *You ask me why.*
17. Walter Lippmann, *A Preface to Morals,* page 233. (Macmillan.)
18. See, for example, *The Iron Man in Industry,* by Arthur Pound. (Little, Brown.)
19. John Herman Randall, Jr., *Our Changing Civilization,* page 181. (Stokes.)
20. Luke 15:7.
21. John Masefield, *Invocation,* included in *Collected Poems.* Used by permission of The Macmillan Company, publishers.

22. Robert Browning, *Pauline*.
23. William Shakespeare, *Macbeth*.
24. John Masefield, *The Everlasting Mercy*, included in *The Everlasting Mercy, and The Widow in the Bye Street*. Used by permission of The Macmillan Company, publishers.
25. Frederic W. H. Myers, *Saint Paul*, included in *Collected Poems*. Used by permission of The Macmillan Company, publishers.
26. Henry Dwight Sedgwick, *Pro Vita Monastica*, page 15. (Atlantic Monthly Press.)
27. *Ian Maclaren, the Life of John Watson*, page 117, by W. Robertson Nicoll. (Dodd.)
28. I am almost sure I am indebted for this phrase to George Matheson, though a search has not revealed it in his writings.
29. Luke 9:23.
30. An incident related in *When Faiths Flash Out*, chap. I, by David Baines-Griffiths. (Revell.)
31. II Corinthians 4:6.

CHAPTER VI

THE CRAFTSMANSHIP OF THE PREACHER

1. Frederic W. H. Myers, *Saint Paul*, included in *Collected Poems*. Used by permission of The Macmillan Company, publishers.
2. Joseph Fort Newton, *The New Preaching*, page 116. (Cokesbury Press.)
3. Richard Watson Gilder, *How to the Singer Comes the Song?* Included in *The World's Great Religious Poetry*, edited by Caroline M. Hill. (Macmillan.)
4. James Black, *The Mystery of Preaching*, page 72. (Revell.)

5. John Kelman, *The War and Preaching,* page 108. (Yale University Press.)
6. II Corinthians 11:3. The American Version gives the correct translation.
7. Matthew 7:24–27.
8. Matthew 11:28.
9. Luke 12:57.
10. Ephesians 4:26.
11. John Ruskin, *Modern Painters,* vol. III, part iv, chap. xvi, § 28.
12. A. Hamilton Gibbs, *Soundings.* (Little, Brown.)
13. Matthew 12:36.
14. John Drinkwater, *Reciprocity.* Used by permission of Houghton Mifflin Company.
15. S. Parkes Cadman, *Ambassadors of God,* page 262. (Macmillan.)
16. A. J. Gossip, *In Christ's Stead,* page 180. (Doran.)
17. *Ibid.,* page 223.
18. I John 1:1–4.

CHAPTER VII

THE PERSONALITY OF THE PREACHER

1. John Milton, *Apology for Smectymnuus.*
2. Francis Thompson, *The Hound of Heaven.*
3. John 1:14.
4. Frederic W. H. Myers, *Saint Paul,* included in *Collected Poems.* Used by permission of The Macmillan Company, publishers.
5. I Corinthians 15:41.
6. This story is given in *The Message and the Man* by J. Dodd Jackson. (Hammond.) The book has considerable denominational coloring, but is nevertheless of much value to the preacher.

7. Leviticus 19:18, Luke 10:27.

8. John 6:63.

9. Luke 1:3.

10. John 1:6.

11. John 4:29.

12. W. Fearon Halliday, *Psychology and Religious Experience*, page 128.   (R. R. Smith.)

13. Matthew 9:29.

14. Mark 5:36, Luke 8:50, Mark 9:23.

15. John Masefield, *The Everlasting Mercy*, included in *The Everlasting Mercy, and The Widow in the Bye Street*. Used by permission of The Macmillan Company, publishers.

16. *The Message and the Man*, page 95, by J. Dodd Jackson (Hammond), gives a feeling description of this incident.

17. II Corinthians 2:16.

18. John Watson, *The Cure of Souls*, page 227. (Dodd.)

19. Psalm 97:11.

20. A contention convincingly made in *Creative Prayer*, page 139, by E. Herman. (Doran.)

21. John 21:25.

22. Luke 15:20.

23. William Wordsworth, *Expostulation and Reply*.

24. Matthew 19:13.

25. Luke 22:32.

26. John 17:15.

27. John 17:20.

28. Luke 23:34.

29. Alexander Whyte, *Lord, Teach Us to Pray*, pp. 51 f.

30. *Ibid.*

31. Robert Browning, *Instans Tyrannus*.

32. Hebrews 2:3.

CHAPTER VIII

THE PREACHING OF THE CROSS

1. Revelation 5:9.
2. I Corinthians 2:2.
3. Galatians 6:14.
4. Quoted in the chapter by Hu Shih in *Whither Mankind?* edited by Charles A. Beard. (Longmans.)
5. George Stewart, *The Crucifixion in our Street*. (R. R. Smith.)
6. Quoted in *The Meaning of the Cross*, page 7, by Henry Sloane Coffin. (Scribners.)
7. Deuteronomy 21:22.
8. M. L. Fisher, *On a Sculptured Head of the Christ*. Included in *Sonnets: A First Series* (New York, 1917). Used by permission.
9. Matthew 16:23, Mark 8:33.
10. John 10:18.
11. Mark 8:34.
12. John 12:32.
13. C. Bodin, *Dream No More*. Included in *Redemption, An Anthology of the Cross*, page 286, edited by George Stewart. (R. R. Smith.)
14. Edwin Arlington Robinson, *Calvary*, included in *The Children of the Night*. Used by permission of Charles Scribner's Sons.
15. I Samuel 25:29.
16. Alice Meynell, *Christ in the Universe*, included in *Poems*. (Scribners.)
17. *Go, Bitter Christ*, an anonymous poem included in *Redemption, An Anthology of the Cross*, page 307, edited by George Stewart. (R. R. Smith.)
18. Matthew 6:24, Luke 16:13.
19. Alfred Tennyson, *Maud*.

20. Quoted in the *Expositor's Dictionary of Texts,* vol. I,
     page 1015. (Doran.)
21. Matthew 10:39.
22. Matthew 18:8, 9; Mark 9:43-47.
23. Matthew 10:28.
24. Henry van Dyke, *Joy and Power,* page 41. (Crowell.)
25. Francis Thompson, *The Hound of Heaven.*
26. H. W. Farrington, *Our Christ.* Included in *Rough and
     Brown* and used by permission.
27. *For All Thy Saints,* the hymn by W. Walsham How.
28. I Corinthians 6:20.
29. *There is a Green Hill,* the hymn by Mrs. C. F. Alex-
     ander.

INDEX

INDEX

251
B98

44876